THE

GATHERING

OF THE WATERS

A New Discussion
of the Lost Tribes of Israel

THE
GATHERING
OF THE WATERS

A New Discussion
of the Lost Tribes of Israel

by

Clay McConkie

The
Gathering
of the Waters

ISBN 1-56684-253-0

Computer
Carol Brinkerhoff
Cover
John McConkie

Printed by
Publishers Press
Salt Lake City,
Utah

Author

Clay McConkie is a native of Utah. He is a teacher by occupation, having taught in the Salt Lake City Schools for thirty years. He received a B.A. from Brigham Young University and an M.S. and Ph. D. from the University of Utah. His wife is the former Grace Wilson, and they have four children.

Note on Chronology

There are several places in the following account where the chronology of people and events is questionable. Consequently, dates are sometimes stated in a way which reflects more than one point of view. Where differences do exist, however, they usually do not affect the content of the material.

The time period for Noah and the Flood, for example, might differ as much as 800 years or more, yet the information involved remains basically the same.

Generations from Enoch to Adam

Enoch	Enoch was the 4th great-grandson of Adam. He and his city were taken up from the earth when he was 365 years old. (Genesis 5:23-24)
Methuselah	Methuselah was the oldest man on earth and died at the age of 969, apparently during the year of the Flood. (Genesis 5:27)
Lamech	
Noah	The great Flood occurred in the 600th year of Noah's life. (Genesis 7:6 and 11)
Shem	
Arphaxad	
Salah	
Eber	Eber was the ancestor of an important group of people. (Genesis 10:21) He has been referred to as the ancestor and founder of the Hebrews.
Peleg	It was during Peleg's days that the earth was divided. He was the 3rd great-grandson of Noah. (Genesis 10:25)
Reu	
Serug	
Nehor	
Terah	
Abraham	Abraham was the 3rd great-grandson of Peleg. (Genesis 11:26) He in turn was the grandfather of Jacob who became the head of twelve tribes of Israel.

Two Extraordinary Events

One of the dramatic occurrences of the last days, according to the Book of Zechariah in the Bible, will be when the Mount of Olives cleaves into two parts, opening up an avenue of escape for the Jewish people during the Battle of Armageddon. At about the same time, and possibly in much the same way, the legendary ten tribes of Israel will return from the north. Some kind of barrier, such as a mountain of rock and ice, will cleave apart before them, creating a passageway from an unknown region to the outside world!

The predicted event at the Mount of Olives, surrounded by mystery and the supernatural, gives credibility to the idea that the return of the ten tribes will likewise be a miraculous occurrence. There is also the implication that the tribes will be coming from a very unusual place, one far removed from ordinary circumstances. Although some believe they are currently living a normal kind of life and will someday reappear in a conventional manner, the evidence appears otherwise. What little is known about this mysterious group of people points more toward events and phenomena that are extremely extraordinary!

TABLE OF CONTENTS

LIST OF ILLUSTRATIONS

Figure

PREFACE

One of my purposes in writing this book has been to give an opinion and to express a viewpoint. I have tried to say a few things that possibly have not been said before, and in doing so, maybe I have made some kind of contribution.

Purposely, I have tried to stay away from a bibliography. Instead of summarizing outside information or quoting what others have said, my intent mostly has been to give my own personal ideas. Aside from a very few sources, most of the quotes and references are from the scriptures.

In the process of writing, I have also tried not to be presumptuous. A professor in college gave me some good advice once when he wrote a marginal note on one of my papers, saying that "a little humility and modest restraint would be charming." I have tried to remember that in this book, although maybe not enough sometimes.

There is also the matter of repetition. It often occurs, but hopefully with the effect of better emphasizing a point or promoting an idea.

Finally, and most important, I have attempted not only to put across a viewpoint but to encourage appreciation for the main subject of my material. I believe it is vital, in other words, to view the ten tribes from a new perspective and, above all, to reinforce the idea that they definitely exist! My purpose has also been to reaffirm two basic principles of faith which underlie everything that is set forth in this book, namely the divinity of Jesus Christ and the reality of his second coming. If I have done these things, I will have accomplished my objective.

The thought has also occurred to me from time to time that I might be right, and that the theories contained in these pages are actually correct! I do not say this presumptuously, but only with the idea that in some way I have possibly happened upon a few of the right answers in regard to the lost tribes of Israel. There is a good chance, I think, that this might turn out to be true.

INTRODUCTION

Twice during the world's recorded history, according to the Bible, there has been a dramatic change in the surface of the earth due to a gigantic reduction or displacement of water. The first of these was at the time of Creation as described in the first chapter of Genesis. The other was in the days of Noah following the great Flood.

As a sequel to these two changes, another is yet to come, one scheduled to occur in the last days when the final religious prophecies begin to be fulfilled. This third and momentous event will again diminish the seas and oceans and restore the earth to a condition that existed several thousand years ago.

All three of these events are directly connected to a "gathering together of the waters" on a huge scale and one that is often difficult to imagine. It is easy to read about such things in scripture and say they are true, but to try to visualize what actually happened, and also how it will happen again, is another matter.

First of all, such occurrences are associated with an almost unbelievable amount of liquid territory. One has only to recall what it was like making a surface crossing of the ocean for the first time to get a small indication of how much water is involved.

And then to think of a large percentage of this vast area being gathered together is equally incredible. Imagining how it would take place, and accepting it as fact, requires not only an act of intellect but an exercise of faith as well.

It is much like visualizing the parting of the Red Sea, with a wall of water on each side, and also comprehending what

Joshua did when he commanded the sun and moon to stand still. Both of these might be considered as natural phenomena in some ways, yet in comparison with everyday events and the normal course of things, they are definitely part of the supernatural.

But that is one of the good things about being a Christian! There are so many miracles to believe in, and many more still to come. And the more unbelievable a phenomenon or event might appear sometimes, the more potential it might actually have of being true and significant. A good example, of course, was in the very beginning when God created the heaven and the earth.

THE CREATION

During the first three days of Creation, as recorded in the Book of Genesis, major changes occurred on the earth's surface. "And the earth was without form, and void; and darkness was upon the face of the deep. And the Spirit of God moved upon the face of the waters."

"And God said, Let the waters under the heaven be gathered together unto one place, and let the dry land appear: and it was so. And God called the dry land Earth; and the gathering together of the waters called he Seas: and God saw that it was good." [1]

The implication in this scripture is that the outside of the earth originally was nothing but a vast ocean. Then came the command for reducing or displacing a huge amount of water in order to create land surfaces. In other words, the waters were gathered together. This was a tremendous undertaking, one that might have lasted several months or longer if compared with the great Flood in Noah's time, or even millions of years according to a broader view, and it brings up an inevitable question. And that is, what happened to the large volume of ocean that disappeared or that was possibly relocated?

A supernatural event in which water simply vanished could be the answer. When Jesus fed the five thousand, for example, there was a miraculous multiplication of food, and according to some kind of reverse principle, either food or water might also be miraculously reduced.

Another possibility is that widespread sinking terrain occurred, allowing water to rush into the low places and at the same time causing surrounding landforms to appear. This sounds like Isaiah when he said the mountains and hills would be made low and the rough places plain. Such an occurrence, however, would result in water displacement only, rather than any kind of reduction, unless much of the water flushed down into underground areas of the earth.

Still another possible answer exists. It is first suggested in Genesis where water is referred to as gathering unto one place. Of course, *one place* could mean that all the water ended up in one area and the land in another, yet there might also be a second interpretation, or at least a double meaning. Along with the Creation account, a strong implication is given elsewhere in scripture that a tremendous volume of ocean was actually drawn to a specific geographical location somewhere in the north, after which a uniform sea level, by some type of natural phenomenon, was established and maintained.

This last idea at first might seem unlikely and impractical, even inconsistent or supernatural. Yet as things turn out, it could conceivably be closer to the truth than any other theory!

But regardless of what happened to the waters when they were gathered together, an interesting possibility now appears, and that is that following the third day of Creation, there was much less water visible on the earth's surface than at present. This could mean that in those days a huge landmass extended for thousands of miles in every direction, and instead of there being continents and smaller areas of territory like today, the land surface of the globe might well have been one gigantic island!

Such could have been the condition of the earth's geography in the early centuries of recorded history, including the days of Adam, Enoch, and Noah, the main prophets and patriarchs of the antediluvian period. This was a time which covered the approximate years of 4000 to 2350 B.C. according to one chronology, or several centuries earlier according to another, and ended when the prophet Noah was 600 years old. It was also a time, once again, when the earth's land surface might have been located continuously in one place, as were the waters of the sea which had been gathered together. And then came the great Flood!

THE FLOOD

The deluge which inundated the earth at this time appears to have come from two main sources: (1) rainfall and (2) subterranean areas. It seems logical that most of the flooding came from below rather than above, considering the tremendous volume involved, but the important thing is that while it rained for 150 days, water at the same time was coming in from the places underground.

"In the six hundredth year of Noah's life, in the second month, the seventeenth day of the month, the same day were all the fountains of the great deep broken up, and the windows of heaven were opened." "And the waters prevailed upon the earth an hundred and fifty days."

Then both the rain and underground flooding came to an end. "The fountains also of the deep and the windows of heaven were stopped, and the rain from heaven was restrained; and the waters returned from off the earth continually: and after the end of the hundred and fifty days the waters were abated." [2]

Whether or not the earth was completely submerged in water has been debated, but the biblical record does state that all the high hills and also the mountains were covered, and that all living things upon the earth were killed. Although there are other reasons given in support of complete inundation, these two are the traditional ones.

No reference is made to any natural phenomena that contributed to the Flood except rainfall and the underground sources of water. If there were any, at least they are not mentioned specifically in the Bible. [3] It was mainly a matter of a huge release of water that possibly came and went in much the same way.

One thing is certain. The giant deluge during the time of Noah was one of the most dramatic events in human history, and the subsequent withdrawal of water, during a period of about five and a half months, was in some ways no less spectacular.

The old saying that what goes up must come down is especially true of the Flood. But an important question is whether or not the water went back the same way it came. So far there is no definite answer, but logic once again would say yes. And if this is true, it establishes a process or principle that can be used in connection with the two other great events: the one during the Creation and also an event still to occur in the future.

This process of water action consists of two parts. Part One during the Flood was water coming by rainfall and from underground sources. Part Two was the water returning to those sources, or in other words, gathering the waters together and causing the dry land to appear.

The underground sources, of course, according to the Bible, were the unusual phenomenon known as the fountains of the great deep.

FOUNTAINS OF THE DEEP

There are many biblical events that have to be classed as miracles, things unexplainable by any scientific principle. Jesus raising people from the dead and also walking on water were definitely supernatural occurrences. And even though it is a good idea to look for a natural explanation of things whenever possible, going along with science instead of refuting it, still this is not always easy to do with certain events and phenomena in the Bible.

One such example is the fountains of the deep. Along with scientific explanations that might be given, there is something unusual enough about this subject of nature to class it at least partially in the category of the supernatural.

In the Bible there are only a few places where *fountains of the deep* or *fountains of the great deep* are mentioned, but the location and function of this mysterious area make it extremely important. First, it was evidently the main source of water during the Flood. The world record for rainfall in one day is 73.6 inches, and if that figure is multiplied by 150 days of rain time, it amounts to 920 feet. Using this total as an approximation of rainwater involved, it appears obvious that the remaining quantity of water necessary to cover even a few of the hills and mountains of the earth would be much higher. A tremendous amount would have had to come from subterranean sources.

Second, the fountain outlets might have been at any number of places on the ocean floor, or even on land surfaces, but more particularly, depending on scriptural interpretation, at one specific geographical location. This has been designated in modern scripture as a region in the northern

Figure 1

World Records for Rainfall

World

One Day	73.62 inches March 15 and 16, 1952 Cilaos, La Reunion, Indian Ocean
One Month	366 inches July, 1861 Cherrapunji, Meghalaya, India
One Year	1,041.8 inches August 1, 1860 to July 31, 1861 Cherrapunji, Meghalaya, India

United States

One Day	19 inches July 25 and 26, 1979 Alvin, Texas
One Year	739 inches December, 1981 to December, 1982 Kukui, Maui, Hawaii
One Year	184.56 inches Continental United States 1931 Wynoochee Oxbow, Washington

*Peter Matthews (Editor), *The Guinness Book of Records, 1994* (New York: Guinness Publishing Company, 1993), p. 23.

---

part of the globe. [4] It could be the same general area as the *north country* or the *land of the north* spoken of by Jeremiah, and the place also where the lost tribes of Israel disappeared many centuries ago.

Third, in the same place in modern scripture, as well as in the Bible, the fountains seem to be given an equal status with three other great creations: the heavens, the earth, and the sea. "And the servants of God shall go forth, saying with a loud voice: Fear God and give glory to him, for the hour of his judgment is come; and worship him that made heaven, and earth, and the sea, and the fountains of waters." [5]

The term *fountains of waters* here might possibly be interpreted as a variety of water features on the earth's surface, including rivers, lakes and streams. And yet the fact that it appears along with three creations of the greatest importance suggests that it is much more than that.

There is a certain bumper sticker containing the names of Paris, New York, London, Tokyo and Moab, listed in that order. By comparison, to list the fountains of waters as a fourth type of creation, defining the term merely as water features of the earth, would be to express things in much the same way. A more logical conclusion is that this object of nature constitutes more of a major entity, along with heavens, earth and sea, and is synonymous with the fountains of the great deep in the Bible.

Although much might be said about subterranean water, therefore, geologically and otherwise, the important implication in scripture is that somewhere it does exist! And if the account of the Flood in the Bible is to be taken seriously, it evidently exists in mammoth proportions!

Also it has the potential of significantly affecting the earth's geology. When the fountains of the great deep were broken up during the time of Noah, for example, it were as though all nature had broken loose, and not only was the earth inundated with water, but huge changes in the land surface possibly took place as well.

Moreover, this same thing might have been true a century or so later, although obviously to a much lesser degree, when another outstanding event occurred. It was one that affected the lives of relatively very few people when it happened, yet one also that eventually produced worldwide consequences. This was the *division of the earth* mentioned in the Bible and coincided with the birth of a very obscure figure in history--a man by the name of Peleg!

THE DAYS OF PELEG

Peleg was a 3rd great-grandson of Noah and according to the biblical record was born about one hundred years after the Flood. This was a time period when a third deluge appears to have taken place, one comparable in some ways to the great Flood itself, but of lesser magnitude and close enough in time that it caused less attention and publicity. The Bible speaks of it only briefly, and the chronology involved might be inaccurate, yet it was evidently an occurrence of great intensity and importance, for because of it in the time of Peleg, the land surface of the earth was divided!

It was an event distinctive enough that it prompted Peleg's name, which in the Hebrew language signifies *watercourse* and *division*. Something of great significance occurred in those days, and he was named after it. In a similar way, Mark Twain might have been named Haley because he was born at the same time the famous comet appeared.

There are only two places in the Bible where a specific division of the earth is mentioned. In the Book of Genesis, for example, the following brief account is recorded: "And unto Eber were born two sons: the name of one was Peleg; for in his days was the earth divided; and his brother's name was Joktan." [6] The same account, with a minor change in wording, appears in the First Book of Chronicles.

And that is it! Nothing more is said about it. Yet for such a momentous event, if that is what it turns out to be, this *division of the earth* could be the most unpublicized occurrence in the Bible. It is almost as if it were a fact purposely caused to be hidden, something like the City of Enoch or the ten lost tribes of Israel.

But what does it mean when it says the earth was divided? Was there an actual geological or geographical division, or does it refer mainly to something else such as agricultural improvements or a redistribution of people? Certainly these are questions that have prompted a variety of answers, some dealing mostly with land, others with water, and still others referring almost exclusively to population.

In connection with this ambiguous event, therefore, which is possibly related to the fountains of the deep and the gathering of waters, there are at least six ways in which it might be explained. One, it was a vast separation of people, both linguistically and geographically, at the time of the Tower of Babel. Two, there was an important development in agriculture and cultivation in the Mesopotamian area, including the use of artificial irrigation canals.

Three, a division took place in which land and territory were separated into districts. Four, it was the conclusion of the Flood that occurred in the time of Noah, completing the configuration of land surfaces as they appear today. Five, this was the period in history when the continents drifted apart. And finally, it was a time when water again inundated the earth, on a separate occasion from the Flood, enough to cause an immense amount of territory and land forms to disappear.

All of these theories are important, of course, but once again very different, and it is the etymology of Peleg's name that should provide a clue to the right answer. When the concepts of *watercourse* and *division* are viewed together, for example, it seems logical that they suggest more than a linguistic and geographical division of people, improvements in agricultural techniques, or the establishment of municipal boundaries and districts. Much more than these appears to be intended. Also there are good reasons for rejecting the idea that the division of the earth was merely the final phase of the great Flood. (See Figure 16.)

When all of these possibilities are set aside, therefore, only two alternatives remain: continental drift and the additional inundation of land by water.

The continental drift theory, first of all, states that the lower half of Africa's western coast at one time adjoined the eastern coast of South America, and also that the rest of Africa connected mainly with the eastern part of North America. Other parts of the earth were joined together in a similar way, all forming one landmass. Then came a time when large sections of land started drifting apart to form continents, continuing to do so until they arrived at the condition in which they appear today. And although this theory got off to a shaky start, with its main advocate being criticized and ridiculed by the scientific community, it now exists as a generally accepted concept under the name of plate tectonics.

There is a time problem, however, in associating the drifting continents with what happened during the days of Peleg. Scientists estimate that the continents started moving 200 to 300 million years ago, whereas Bible chronologists often place Peleg's time at about 2250 B.C., or possibly a few centuries earlier. Of course, it could be said that science has been wrong before and in this case is wrong again, but in regard to this particular situation, it might be well to avoid conflict between a biblical event and such a well-known scientific idea. Besides, another option definitely exists!

In addition to the drifting continents concept, there is a sixth possible explanation, one that is supported by scripture and at the same time is relatively acceptable in terms of science. It is the idea of water coming in upon the earth via rainfall and underground sources, at least one of these and maybe both, inundating large areas of land and causing a division of territory. It is the same kind of process that occurred during the Flood, except that the floodwaters abated at an earlier time. Such a phenomenon, which is plausible as well as possible, is much more likely to avoid an unnecessary confrontation between scientific theory and the Bible.

The main clue as to what actually happened is found once again in modern scripture, in an account predicting certain events still to occur in the future. It is only a brief comment, much like the biblical reference to Peleg, yet it suggests very strongly what occurred when the earth was divided, and also

Figure 2

DRIFTING CONTINENTS

Piecing together the parts of a world map might give a general idea of what the earth looked like more than 200 million years ago after the continents started drifting apart.

Alfred Wegener, the man who brought the continental drift theory into prominence, gave his concept of the original landmass the name of *Pangaea*. A view of this is depicted in Figure 15.

---

how things will eventually be restored by a reverse principle to their original condition. The scripture pertains to the second coming of Christ.

"He shall command the great deep, and it shall be driven back into the north countries, and the islands shall become one land; and the land of Jerusalem and the land of Zion shall be turned back into their own place, and the earth shall be like as it was in the days before it was divided." [7]

Such a piece of information provides important insight and also clears up a lot of questions. First, the division of the earth during Peleg's time was mainly the result of incoming water, a huge deluge which caused a separation of land into islands and continents. There was no quick version of a continental drift, nor was there any need for one, although significant geological changes might still have taken place on the earth's surface.

Second, water driven *back* into the north countries is an implication that that is where it came from in the first place during the days of Peleg, originating somewhere in the northern part of the globe. It came down out of the north, and it will go back into the north. Within this context, water gathered together unto *one place*, as found in the Creation account, takes on additional meaning.

Third, it is an important discovery to find the meaning of the word "divided" as it is recorded in the tenth chapter of Genesis. There appears to be considerable evidence now that it refers to one of three great deluges in human history, with Peleg as its namesake!

Finally, the division of the earth was a spiritual occurrence, as well as one that was physical. In other words, a divine command undoubtedly was given which set this unusual event into motion. It initiated Part One in which water flooded the earth during the early days of Peleg, and it will also initiate Part Two in the future when the waters of the great deep again will be driven back into the north countries.

These kinds of occurrences, of course, are not without parallel and precedence in scripture. One example, especially in regard to the seas and oceans, is found in the Book of Proverbs where *Wisdom* is personified and speaks out in a woman's voice. "The Lord possessed me in the beginning of his way," she said, "before his works of old. I was set up from everlasting, from the beginning, or ever the world was. When there were no depths, I was brought forth; when there were no fountains abounding with water."

"When he prepared the heavens, I was there: when he set a compass upon the face of the depth: when he established the clouds above: when he strengthened the fountains of the deep: when he gave to the sea his decree, that the waters should not pass his commandment." [8]

The references in Proverbs are interesting, especially those pertaining to a decree and the fountains of the deep. These scriptures reinforce the idea that events and physical phenomena which are of great magnitude, and which significantly affect the lives of mankind, often do not happen merely by chance or according to natural causes but occur at a specific time and place as the result of a divine command.

Certainly they are things that have occurred all down through history, having an important effect on many different nations and people. They have had a determining influence on a long series of civilizations. And although their significance might not always have been apparent at the time, they nevertheless have had far-reaching consequences.

Such was particularly true in connection with a large colony of Israelites who lived in northern and central Palestine, some of whom were eventually separated from their kinsmen during invasions and later became known as the ten lost tribes of Israel. Indeed it was this latter group, surrounded by mysterious circumstances and uncertainty, that was involved in a very strange episode in ancient history, and one also that allegedly had an unexpected relationship with the third deluge and a future gathering of the waters!

THE TEN TRIBES

Seven generations after the time of Peleg and the dramatic division of the earth, a man named Jacob was born. This was Abraham's grandson, also known as Israel, who became the originator and head of the twelve tribes that bore his name.

It was Jacob who was the grand progenitor of the House of Israel, a group of people that spent 430 years in Egyptian bondage, later journeyed to the promised land in Palestine, and one day became a large nation under the kings Saul, David and Solomon. The united house came to an end, however, in the 10th Century B.C. when the Israelites quarreled among themselves and divided into two separate groups.

The tribe of Judah and part of the tribe of Benjamin went in one direction, while the remaining tribes, including the other part of Benjamin, went in another. One became known as the Kingdom of Judah with its capital at Jerusalem, and the other the Kingdom of Israel with a capital farther north, first at Shechem and Tirzah and later in Samaria. Both were eventually conquered by invading armies and taken into captivity.

It was the Kingdom of Israel, however, that was marked for a strange and unusual destiny. Two hundred years or more after becoming a separate entity, it fell prey to the Assyrians who uprooted a large part of the population and transported it to various parts of the Assyrian Empire. This was the group referred to as the ten tribes.

Then came the period of history when at least some of these people finally gathered together again and embarked on a historic journey, one that took them deep into the north

Figure 3

The Twelve Sons of Israel

Jacob, or Israel, had four wives, and by them he had twelve sons and a daughter.

Leah
1. Reuben
2. Simeon   Genesis 29:32-35
3. Levi
4. Judah

Bilhah
5. Dan   Genesis 30:6-8
6. Naphtali

Zilpah
7. Gad   Genesis 30:10-13
8. Asher

Leah
9. Issachar   Genesis 30:17-21
10. Zebulun
      Dinah

Rachel
11. Joseph   Genesis 30:22-24
12. Benjamin   35:16-18

Each son except Joseph became the head of a tribe. Joseph's two sons Ephraim and Manasseh were also tribe leaders, which brought the total number to thirteen. Because of a religious calling, however, those under Levi were not included among the traditional twelve tribes.

All of these groups together, united under Jacob's leadership, became known in biblical history as the House of Israel.

Figure 4

Kings of Israel and Judah

Sometime during the 10th Century B.C., following the time of Saul, David, and Solomon, the House of Israel was divided into two separate kingdoms.

Kingdom of Israel	Kingdom of Judah
Jeroboam I	Rehoboam
Nadab	Abijam
Baasha	Asa
Elah	Jehoshaphat
Zimri	Jehoram
Omri	Ahaziah
Ahab	Athaliah
Ahaziah	Joash
Jehoram	Amaziah
Jehu	Uzziah
Jehoahaz	Jotham
Jehoash	Ahaz
Jeroboam II	Hezekiah
Zachariah	Manasseh
Shallum	Amon
Menahem	Josiah
Pekahiah	Jehoahaz
Pekah	Jehoiakim
Hoshea	Jehoiachin
	Zedekiah
Nineteen Kings End of Kingdom c. 721 B.C.	Twenty Kings. End of Kingdom c. 587 B.C.

It was during the time of Pekah and Hoshea, kings of Israel, that people from among the ten tribes were taken away into Assyrian captivity.

country. There they mysteriously disappeared, later to become known as the lost tribes of Israel. The only account of this event, very brief in content and uncertain as to authenticity, is found in the Apocrypha. [9]

"But they formed this plan for themselves, that they would leave the multitude of the nations and go to a more distant region, where mankind had never lived, that there at least they might keep their statutes which they had not kept in their own land."

Concerning the route that the tribes followed, the account continues. "And they went in by the narrow passages of the Euphrates River. For at that time the Most High performed signs for them, and stopped the channels of the river until they had passed over. Through that region there was a long way to go, a journey of a year and a half; and that country is called Arzareth." [10]

The apocryphal references to "Arzareth," which in Hebrew means *another land*, and "the narrow passages of the Euphrates River" are the only clues as to where the tribes went. One thing appears certain, however, and that is that their general direction of travel was north, far enough that they could escape from the multitude of nations and find a more distant region where people had never gone before.

The whereabouts and present status of the ten tribes continue to be a mystery, and it has come to be a topic of conversation as to where they might be. It is also a common opinion sometimes that the topic is one that should generally be left alone since it is surrounded by so much conjecture and speculation. In other words, there are more important things to do than talking in circles about the location of the ten tribes.

And yet there is something about this subject that makes it hard to set aside. A lack of knowledge and information can easily turn into bothersome questions, and the only way to get rid of them, if that is possible, is to try to find the answers, or at least form an enlightened opinion, supported by the facts that are available and the best of circumstantial evidence.

There is also the realization that all of this is much more than just a topic of conversation. Definitely it is part of the phenomenon known as the scattering and gathering of Israel. It is the idea that Israelites down through history have been removed to new lands or dispersed among the nations, yet at the same time have been given the promise that they will be gathered again and reunited. And according to religious prophecy, the lost tribes are one of those groups and will someday be restored to their original lands of inheritance.

In the meantime, however, they remain hidden away in some remote and undisclosed area, the only clue as to their location being that they last traveled through a place called Arzareth. This was far removed from their original starting point in Mesopotamia and again might have been one of the places Jeremiah referred to when he talked about the "north country" or the "land of the north." Also it is this same part of the globe where a water supply for mammoth floods allegedly exists, along with a rendezvous place for a mysterious gathering of the waters!

LAND OF THE NORTH

Aside from the traditional view of places like Alaska and the Yukon Territory being mystic lands of ice and snow, along with the arctic and polar regions beyond, there is an additional mystery about this northern area. Not only is it the locality associated with the ten tribes of Israel, but it also appears to be a place which has an unusual capacity for a huge output and intake of water!

First, this is where the deluge during the time of Peleg evidently originated, or at least initially appeared on the earth's surface. Water came pouring down from the north like a giant tidal wave, as it were, or more likely in a less dramatic manner, and caused massive changes in the geography. People in those days were obviously aware of at least some of these changes, or they would not have had occasion to give Peleg such an unusual name because of the earth being divided.

Second, if this particular region can be identified as the origin of water for the Peleg deluge, it can also be reasoned to be the one for the Flood during the time of Noah, and even possibly at the time of Creation. Conversely, and according to a reverse process, it would then be the same area where floods would return each time--or in other words, the gathering place of the waters!

"Gather the waters together and cause the dry land to appear!" This divine command was given not only at the beginning of biblical times, but most likely also at the conclusion of the great Flood, and in the future it will again be given when the waters of the great deep are driven back into the north countries. Consequently, it gives added significance to the land of the north and establishes it as a main focal point for some of the most dramatic events in human history.

Yet if this is true, and if this is the way things really are, the question again is raised as to where a tremendous amount of water goes when it is gathered together. Does it miraculously disappear in a way comparable to certain miracles in the Bible? Does it fill into large areas of sinking terrain? Or is it actually gathered together unto one place and then absorbed and engineered into other areas of the earth?

In a deluge, water comes from an outside source, or is the result of some kind of displacement, raising the sea level and spreading out across the land. During a reverse action, however, when the water returns or is *driven back* to its original place, something has to happen to it in order for a normal sea level to be maintained.

Of the three phenomena, therefore, which offer a possible explanation--a miraculous disappearance of water, sinking terrain, or water being absorbed into the earth--the last one could well be the closest to the truth. For one thing, it would eliminate the necessity of huge geologic changes on the earth's surface, although some of these might still occur. Also it would keep things in a more realistic perspective as far as the normal course of things is concerned.

But is it plausible, or even possible, for gigantic volumes of water to appear and disappear in some area of the north countries? Can events like these be regarded as realistic, or do they have to be viewed more in terms of the supernatural? Actually, the right answer could be a little of both.

Geologists would agree with a certain amount of subterranean water in a variety of forms, but anything comparable to an underground sea or ocean might be a different matter. One fact has to be dealt with, however, and that is that during the first two deluges, a large quantity of water came from somewhere, and if not from underground sources, the question is where.

Another problem has to do with the fountains of the deep. Are these fountains, for example, related to the giant movements of water in the north suggested by modern scripture?　Are they responsible for the floods which apparently come and go in that area, possibly in or around the arctic and polar regions?

Although the Flood account in the Bible is brief, still it is very impressive when it says that "all the fountains of the great deep were broken up." This could definitely result in a lot of water, especially during a period of one hundred and fifty days.

All of this might suggest different things, of course, but there is a strong implication in scripture that the fountains of the great deep have an outlet and inlet located somewhere in the north, at a point where floods begin and then eventually go back again. And if all the deluges are viewed together within this context, it appears that the pattern for one of them could well be the pattern for all.

This possibility is especially significant in regard to a third and final deluge, along with the division of the earth, because at the same time in history when the last floodwaters recede, sometime in the latter days, it will then be the predicted time also for the ten tribes to reappear in the very same area!

THE PHENOMENON OF THE TRIBES

It is an interesting parallel that two momentous events in the future will occur at about the same time, both taking place in the north country. When the command is given, for example, for the waters of the great deep to be driven northward, the lost tribes of Israel, after many centuries of isolation, will finally be coming out of the north and heading southward.

"He shall command the great deep, and it shall be driven back into the north countries, and the islands shall become one land."

"And they who are in the north countries shall come in remembrance before the Lord; and their prophets shall hear his voice, and shall no longer stay themselves; and they shall smite the rocks, and the ice shall flow down at their presence. And an highway shall be cast up in the midst of the great deep." [11]

Once again, in referring to material contained in the scriptures, it is not a bad idea to keep things in harmony with the principles of science as much as possible. A good way to lose credibility, in other words, is to try to explain too many things by way of miracles and divine intervention. Most phenomena can actually be viewed in terms of natural law and natural causes. Yet in regard to the return of the lost tribes, there appears to be no way that a completely normal explanation can be given.

The conditions surrounding this great latter-day event will evidently be far removed from any ordinary circumstances. In fact, the things which have been predicted will exceed even the biblical exodus of the Israelites from Egypt, including the dramatic crossing of the Red Sea.

"Therefore, behold, the days come, saith the Lord, that it shall no more be said, The Lord liveth, that brought up the children of Israel out of the land of Egypt; but the Lord liveth, that brought up the children of Israel from the land of the north, and from all the lands whither he had driven them: and I will bring them again into their land that I gave unto their fathers." [12]

The emergence of the lost tribes, therefore, from the mystical land of the north which has held them for so long will consist of not just one miracle but several. And this in turn suggests that the conditions surrounding the tribes themselves, their present status and location, are likewise associated with miraculous circumstances.

As to where the tribes might actually be, the most common opinion according to one survey that has been taken is expressed in a so-called Dispersion Theory. Out of more than 200 people who were polled, fifty-three percent said they thought the tribes were presently dispersed among the nations of the world and that their gathering was now taking place through missionary work.

Another view, the Unknown Planet Theory, was that the tribes occupy a position much like the City of Enoch, in that they have been transported to another planet or sphere. Twenty-nine percent favored this idea.

Eleven percent of the people believed in a North Pole Theory, a view placing the tribes in some kind of hidden area in the polar regions. Also four percent accepted the possibility of a hollow earth, and two percent gave a personal theory of their own. [13]

Whether one or the other of these theories is closer to the truth is undoubtedly a subject for debate, and yet in some ways also relatively unimportant. The main facts involved are that the tribes do actually exist somewhere and that someday they will return. Everything else is mostly opinion and speculation. Concerning a dispersion among the nations, however, which seems to be the most prevalent view, the evidence generally suggests that this particular theory, although a popular one, is very possibly incorrect!

Wherever the tribes are, they appear to be a separate and distinct group, most likely a nation or group of nations, and at least some of them are a religious people. From time to time there have been prophets among them, and these men will someday be given the signal when it is finally time for the tribes to return.

It is the nature of that return, however, that will be very unusual and miraculous, enough so that to hear a description of it in advance might seem unbelievable. Yet at the same time, such a report could also be a verification of its own validity, as well as a valuable clue as to where the tribes are located in the first place!

Again there appears to be no way that a completely rational explanation can be given to identify the whereabouts of the lost tribes of Israel. From the outset, allowances have to be made, especially in this particular situation. The idea must be accepted ahead of time that because of the nature of the subject, miraculous circumstances will undoubtedly be involved.

The present location of the tribes, along with their predicted return, is something that is in the same category as Jesus walking on water, mysteriously appearing and disappearing among people, and rising off the ground into midair. It is the same kind of phenomena as Moses parting the waters of the Red Sea and Joshua causing the sun and moon to stand still. Certainly all of these are remarkable occurrences and are part of the supernatural aspect of scripture which is so characteristic of the Bible!

ROCK, ICE, AND WATER

One line of thinking that might be preparatory to any discussion of the lost tribes is that, with few exceptions, people are pretty well earthbound as far as their existence on this globe is concerned, at least for the time being. They are born here, they die here, and they are buried here, and then they enter the Spirit World which, according to some unknown principle, is also supposed to be here. In addition, the earth will be the scene of the coming Millennium and many important events after that.

Such an idea of a self-contained earth would imply that the ten tribes are at some kind of location having to do with this planet, not off on some other orb or sphere. They are not translated or resurrected beings, like the inhabitants of the City of Enoch, but evidently just ordinary people such as those now living in the various nations.

Also it seems unlikely that the tribes exist somewhere in the polar regions which have been explored up one way and down the other. With a predetermined attitude toward miracles and the supernatural, however, even this might still be regarded as a possibility since the idea of the north countries is such an important factor.

All of this does not leave an awful lot to go by concerning where the tribes are located. There are very few options that remain. And whichever of these might be considered, the same is maybe doomed from the outset because of the unusual circumstances. But there is still another possible solution, and one that could conceivably produce the right answer!

The question was once asked during the course of making a movie as to how it would be best to build a pyramid. Someone suggested that they tear one down that already existed, recording it on film, and then run the movie backwards. Such an idea is humorous, but it is this same kind of process that might be used in trying to describe the situation of the lost tribes.

The verses of modern scripture, for example, which refer to this subject speak of three main elements that will be present when the tribes return: rock, ice, and water. "They shall smite the rocks," the text says, "and the ice shall flow down at their presence. And an highway shall be cast up in the midst of the great deep." [14]

By using this same sequence of events, and then running it through a reverse order, it might be theorized that the ten tribes of Israel, after wandering through an unknown land for a year and a half after their captivity, finally came to a threshold and embarkation point. And in a way similar to what had happened earlier when the waters of the Euphrates River were stopped, they traversed a large expanse of water by way of a highway cast up, arriving at a place where ice flowed down before them and areas of rock and earth gave way to an entrance--a place of entry, in other words, which led to a new land and a final destination!

Inherent in this kind of theory, of course, is immediate skepticism or disbelief. Many would certainly class it in the category of science fiction. They would decry the plausibility of any kind of hollow earth theory or any type of drama resembling a Jules Verne story.

This same attitude, a very natural human reaction, was also the one which existed immediately following the resurrection of Jesus. When Mary Magdalene and other women said they had seen the Lord, the apostles regarded their words as "idle tales" and refused to believe them. After all the miracles they had witnessed in the presence of Jesus, this one was still too much for reasoning men to accept.

Whatever the right answer might be, as far as the disappearance of the ten tribes is concerned, one thing is certain, and that is that their return in the future, at least, will be an eventful one. They might not have disappeared in the same way they will come back, but the statement is clearly given that their return will be miraculous. Besides the drama of ice and rock, the highway will be raised up in the midst of the sea, a way of holiness, as expressed by the prophet Isaiah, and also a literal way of getting out of the north country and starting a long trek southward.

"And an highway shall be there, and a way, and it shall be called the way of holiness; the unclean shall not pass over it; but it shall be for those: the wayfaring men." [15]

In addition, other conditions will surround this great event. Widespread geological changes are predicted, for example, when it says that a divine decree "shall break down the mountains, and the valleys shall not be found." Also some of the land features will be tempered. "And in the barren deserts there shall come forth pools of living water; and the parched ground shall no longer be a thirsty land."

Moreover, as the tribes continue their journey toward a destination far to the south, anyone standing in their way "shall become a prey unto them." [16]

And although such verses of scripture, both biblical and modern, often contain figurative and symbolic language, they also make definite references to geography, enough so that they give meaningful details to Israel's exodus from the north. In other words, the return of the ten tribes now has some important documentation which helps erase some of the mysterious circumstances.

Once again, however, it is not an account of their return that is so much a mystery as it is where they will be coming from in the first place. Where is the legendary location, for example, that presently conceals this elusive group of people? Is there any place at all, which approaches some degree of reasonability, that can possibly explain their mysterious whereabouts? In a final analysis, and in response to these questions, it might be that the gathering of the waters will provide the most valuable clue!

A COMPARISON OF EVENTS

A shroud of mystery covers the two important events that pertain to the north countries or the land of the north. Whether it is the appearance and disappearance of water, or the going and coming of the ten tribes, it is the same. These two phenomena, if they can both be called that, too often deny any reasonable explanation. And yet they exist side by side in several verses of modern scripture.

It has to be more than just coincidence that these two events occur in close proximity to one another. Some kind of meaning or clue must be intended. Something must exist in each one of them that can help solve the puzzle of the other. The occurrence of giant floods, in other words, should help explain various circumstances pertaining to the lost tribes, and vice versa.

There is the phenomenon of water, for one thing, coming out of the north countries and then later receding, or according to scriptural language being *driven back* again. This would imply that somewhere in the northern regions there exists the capacity for a gigantic output and intake of water, enough to accommodate a flood of mammoth proportions. At the same time, it could also suggest a huge subterranean area, including a place of entry and a place of exit for a large group of people.

Both the Bible and modern scripture intimate that a tremendous volume of water does exist beneath the earth's surface, and considering the amount that was involved in the great Flood during the time of Noah, and also the possible deluge during Peleg's time, such a region might comprise not only an underground sea or ocean, but a vast system of lakes and rivers as well. These in turn could suggest a habitat for an extensive population of people and could theoretically be the present location of the ten lost tribes of Israel!

Figure 5

The Gathering Place of the Waters

There are three main areas where the oceans might be *driven back* into the north countries. One is in the North Atlantic between the eastern coast of Greenland and Scandinavia. The others are along the western coast of Greenland, and also in the Pacific, up through the Bering Strait between Siberia and Alaska.

Somewhere beyond these regions is possibly the gathering place of the waters, an area where the earth's giant floods emerge and then recede again.

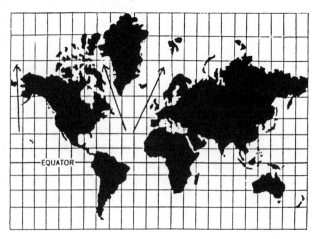

Scientists and geologists, along with the public in general, would possibly refute such a theory or idea at first. Many might also reject the idea that it was a great flood which divided the earth during the days of Peleg, interpreting the word *divided* linguistically, agriculturally, or politically instead. On both of these issues, they would be more apt to accept theories that are more scientifically sound, although maybe at the same time in doing so unintentionally bypassing the truth.

It is not only the unusual qualities pertaining to water, therefore, which give an added dimension to the land of the north but also the disappearance, as well as reappearance, of the ten tribes. This means that somewhere in the north countries there is an area where the tribes were mysteriously swallowed up, as it were, completely disappearing from history and creating from the beginning a very secret situation.

Also the present location of these people, wherever it might be, implies the existence of large amounts of water, possibly comparable in proportion to what the people of the earth are accustomed to. In fact, it could be that a huge recession of water into a subterranean area, spreading floods across the land, might occur at about the same time in the future that the tribes finally start their return.

All of this, of course, is conjecture and speculation. The reality is that some things cannot be completely interpreted or explained, at least at the present. In the meantime, the best possible theories are proposed in anticipation that one of them will turn out to be the truth.

Because of the unique circumstances of this particular situation, however, any kind of solution or explanation that is too simplistic runs the risk of not being true at all. In addition, there is the idea once again that the more unbelievable a phenomenon or event might at first appear, the more potential it might actually have of being significantly important and true.

Certainly there has to be a specific reason why the lost tribes have remained undetected for so many centuries. If there were any logical answer pertaining to their present status and location, scientists and theologians would probably have found it a long time ago, which suggests that certain types of phenomena are involved that deny any kind of normal explanation. And the same is true with a lot of other things, such as how five thousand people were fed with five loaves of bread and two fishes, or how a man came alive again and walked out of his tomb after being dead four days!

It is not beyond possibility, therefore, that the ten tribes, after traveling through the unknown country called Arzareth, eventually disappeared into a northern area which was in the vicinity of the gathering of waters. Here also were the highway and the place of entry. At this time they crossed over an imaginary line dividing the outside world from one of mystery and uncertainty, yet a real one nevertheless, even though at present undetected and not understood.

Their journey very likely took them on a course which allowed for a gradual transition from one geographical area to another. Anyone following this kind of route, if it were ever opened up to him, would maybe be unaware that anything was unusually strange or different. The sea on one side of the line, for example, would be much like that on the other. The same would be true with rivers and lakes, mountains and valleys, and any number of geographical features.

As to the entry itself, however, it very possibly included a dramatic encounter with the elements. Once again the Most High performed signs for the tribes and opened up a way where they could pass through, ice flowing down in front of them, and the rocks crumbling. At such a time all nature would seem to be in commotion. Those witnessing the event would undoubtedly be very impressed, as well as fearful, much like the ancient children of Israel as they watched the parting waters of the Red Sea.

Indeed, this was an occurrence unparalleled in the world's history. Never had this kind of thing ever happened before.

The setting, the circumstances, and the legendary people involved were all part of a unique and spectacular drama that appears to have been associated in some way with an area beneath the surface of the earth.

And if this is true, if this is what actually took place, it could help explain not only the mystery of the lost tribes of Israel, but the fountains of the deep and the gathering of waters as well. Moreover, it would provide a sequel to an important aspect of biblical history and, in the process, add one more item to the long list of Christian miracles which already exists!

THINGS BENEATH THE EARTH

If the nations of the ten tribes have been restricted to the confines of the earth, according to some kind of order or natural law, it means they are living in an unknown geographical location pertaining to this planet. Also if water comes from somewhere in the north, enough to flood the earth and then go back again, some kind of vast underground area must exist which would accommodate this type of activity. The theory is advanced, therefore, that these two phenomena and events--the tribes and the subterranean source of water--both generally have to do with the same place!

This implies that in the last days, when the earth is restored to the way it was before it was divided, the tribes will be coming out of the north at about the same time that receding waters are going in. In other words, the call for the tribes to return will generally coincide with the waters of the great deep being driven back to where they originated.

To advocate such a theory, once again, is to invite immediate loss of credibility. A miracle is a miracle and can often be accepted as such, but to say that the ten tribes possibly exist as a large nation, or group of nations, in another department of the earth and will someday return by way of the north countries might be asking too much. And yet it is equally challenging to try to visualize the actuality of certain other situations, including an extremely populated Spirit World, also said to be in existence on this planet.

One of the things that could turn out to be significant, especially in regard to a subject as controversial as the lost tribes, again has to do with main groups or categories. A previous example was that of heaven, earth, sea, and the fountains of waters. Still another example, and one very closely related, pertains to things in heaven, things on earth, and things *under the earth*. The third part of this last grouping, referring possibly to whatever might exist at a subterranean location, is particularly interesting. It raises a very provocative idea, which is that human life might exist in this area!

In regard to the plausibility of anything of importance being under the earth except geographical features and low forms of animal life, there are two places in the Bible that contain unusual implications. One of these is in the Book of Revelation.

"And every creature which is in heaven, and on the earth, and *under the earth*, and such as are in the sea, and all that are in them, heard I saying, Blessing and honor, and glory, and power be unto him that sitteth upon the throne, and unto the Lamb for ever and ever." [17]

The reference to creatures under the earth, of course, could be given nothing more than figurative or symbolic meaning. Even a literal interpretation might include only a large variety of animal life that lives below the earth's surface, these being personified and endowed with the power of speech.

In another biblical scripture, however, found in the Book of Philippians, a more specific and detailed meaning is suggested. It is a comment referring to Jesus, saying that eventually everyone will admit that he is the Son of God and the predicted Messiah.

"Wherefore, God also hath highly exalted him, and given him a name which is above every name: that at the name of Jesus every knee should bow, of things in heaven, and things in earth, and *things under the earth*; and that every tongue should confess that Jesus Christ is Lord, to the glory of God the Father." [18]

The reference in this scripture to anything but human beings appears unlikely, at least from one point of view, and if so, the probing question is what is meant by things under the earth, those capable of bowing the knee and confessing that Jesus is the Christ. Admittedly, it is only a short statement, and yet much like the brief references to the fountains of the deep and the division of the earth during Peleg's time, it could express a very significant fact.

It is quite obvious that the Bible is reticent on a number of subjects. There is only one place, for example, where it mentions baptism for the dead, or where it refers to three degrees of glory, along with things that are celestial and terrestrial. Yet both of these scriptures underlie subjects of the greatest importance. And the same might be true with things existing under or beneath the earth.

There is still one more verse, incidentally, one occurring in modern scripture, which contains this same type of material. It also mentions things that are spiritual, as well as temporal, a reference that could suggest not only mortal and resurrected beings, but also those who are in the preexistence and the Spirit World.

"And behold, all things have their likeness, and all things are created and made to bear record of me, both things which are temporal, and things which are spiritual; things which are in the heavens above, and things which are on the earth, and things which are in the earth, and *things which are under the earth*, both above *and beneath*: all things bear record of me." [19]

Again it is a matter of three, and maybe four, main categories in regard to various types of creations, each somewhat equal in status with the others. It is the idea that each one has its own sphere of existence and figures prominently in the large scope of things. Each exists according to natural laws and principles, even though they are not always apparent. But these areas and categories do exist and coexist, just the same, and like other kinds of phenomena which are new and unfamiliar, one of them at first will possibly be unacceptable to many people.

Although part of this scripture might pertain to a place like the Spirit World, another part could refer to an area or level of existence, wherever it happens to be, that includes the lost tribes. Regarding this particular category, it all depends on what is meant by things which are under the earth, both above and beneath.

If things *under the earth* do include human beings, as well as other forms of creation, it introduces a very controversial idea. Yet it is one that should be considered, especially in light of the unusual scripture found in Philippians. It is also one that does not have to express the ultraliberal view that people are living in a huge cavity of the earth, one that exists in place of the mantle and core, but more likely a different concept which is much more conservative.

And yet, once again, there is just no way of proposing such a theory, conservative or otherwise, without alienating many of those who hear it. Not only does it appear at first glance to be geologically unsound, but very often impractical and unrealistic.

But then so are many other things that pertain to the Christian religion! This last fact always has to be kept in mind, as do the unusual conditions surrounding the ten tribes and their disappearance in the north country.

The account of the tribes right up to the time that they passed through the land of Arzareth is one that seems historically accurate and correct. Their journey could have taken them between the Black and Caspian Seas, for example, and then on up through Russia to some undetermined area in the north. But at the very last, when the alleged highway rose in front of them, and the ice and rock broke down in order to afford some kind of entrance, the situation immediately changed and took on different circumstances, the type which are much harder to visualize and accept. And some of the events which possibly followed were in turn no less difficult!

THE HOLLOW EARTH THEORY

One method of trying to explain the whereabouts of the ten lost tribes is by way of the Hollow Earth Theory. According to Raymond Bernard, one of its main proponents, the inside of the earth is mostly hollow except for a surface layer of several hundred miles. This central area is said to be habitable, and the light and energy necessary to sustain life are most likely provided by an internal sun.

In his book called *The Hollow Earth*, which is a well-known work on the subject, Dr. Bernard gives a variety of facts and information in an attempt to establish the plausibility of people living beneath the earth's surface. He believes that a polar opening 1400 miles in diameter provides access to the interior, creating a gradual descent that is virtually unnoticeable. An example of someone traveling such a route, he says, was Admiral Richard E. Byrd who in 1947 flew into the opening at the North Pole and penetrated to a distance of 1700 miles.

The Byrd expedition, mentioned repeatedly in the book, allegedly found some very unusual country. In the place of ice and snow, there were mountains, forests, lakes and rivers, and in addition a strange animal resembling a mammoth. It was an unexpected setting which, despite its location in the far north, contained a relatively warm climate.

There was never any verification of Admiral Byrd's plane trip, however, the reason being, according to Dr. Bernard, that news of the event was probably suppressed by government officials. The concern was that other countries would get involved and try to use an important discovery to their own advantage. Such circumstances as these, of course, do not promote the best of credibility, nor does the fact that the earth's interior is often mentioned in *The Hollow Earth* book as a possible source of flying saucers. [20]

Yet one thing does evolve from this theory, if nothing else, and that is that it draws attention to an idea which has definite implications as far as the ten tribes are concerned. If it can be established, in other words, that the tribes are restricted to this planet, that they are not living in the polar regions or anywhere in the northern part of the globe, and that the main segment of their group was not dispersed among the nations, then it has to be assumed that they are still residing in an area pertaining to the earth and at a location that always needs to be related to the north countries.

The Hollow Earth Theory also develops as least a small degree of possibility for subterranean geography and life forms, contending that science is still unaware of many aspects of the earth's geology--if not unaware sometimes, at least undecided or lacking a consensus.

It was only fifty years ago, for example, that astronomers and earth scientists believed that the earth originally was a cooling ball of fire that had spun off from the sun. Now a more likely theory is that it started out as an accumulation of cool cosmic dust and then began a warming process. The point is that scientific discovery is an ongoing thing, and what is regarded as correct today might quickly change tomorrow.

Scientists themselves many times admit that this is true, one of them being Dr. Seiya Uyeda of the University of Tokyo. "It is common to find," he says, "that hypotheses once considered to be reasonably sound to the first order of approximation are in fact fraught with unresolved difficulties." He believes that certain widely-accepted theories in connection with plate tectonics and continental drift might be good examples. [21]

Finally, the theory of a hollow earth is an additional reminder that radically new concepts often gain acceptance very slowly, if at all. Survival is especially difficult when controversy is involved. Just as something plausible might turn out to be false, however, something that seems very strange and unreasonable might also turn out to be true. A good example of this is certainly that of continental drift.

During the early part of the century, Alfred Wegener, who was a German meteorologist, introduced his concept of drifting continents. Immediately he became a subject of ridicule in the scientific community. This might have been partly because his profession was apart from the community itself, but a more obvious reason was that the theories he espoused were too much in opposition to what everyone else believed.

His ideas were so radical that any junior member on a college faculty who promoted them could easily have lost his job, and even senior members with tenure might have placed themselves in jeopardy. Too many things were different, and too much was at stake. As one scientist put it in those days, "If we are to believe Wegener's hypothesis, we must forget everything which has been learned in the last 70 years and start all over again." [22]

And that is exactly what happened! Within just a few decades many of the old theories were discarded and different ones put in their place, resulting in not just a new viewpoint but in some ways a completely new science! At the same time, it reemphasized the lesson and idea that something which is regarded as scientifically sound can actually be very tentative and insecure. In contrast, a theory held in derision because it is different and revolutionary might only have to bide its time before finally gaining recognition and approval.

Again all of these things have interesting implications pertaining to the ten lost tribes, especially in regard to their mysterious journey in the north and their eventual disappearance. The theories of continental drift and the hollow earth both provide significant meaning and background for this extraordinary event in history!

ANOTHER DEPARTMENT OF THE EARTH

As the tribes traveled through the north country, possibly sometime during the 7th Century B.C., they allegedly arrived at a point of embarkation. They had not just traveled there, but they had been led there! They had reached a predetermined rendezvous point where the next stage of their journey could then begin.

It was also at this time that things necessarily took on supernatural circumstances. In order for the tribes to disappear, and to remain hidden from the rest of the world, something apart from the ordinary needed to occur. No one knows what happened, of course, but judging from the few clues that have been given, some kind of entrance way was opened up before them.

This theoretically consisted of three parts: First, a highway appeared, enabling them to traverse a certain expanse of water. Second, some type of phenomenon occurred in which ice flowed down before them. Third, there was an opening in the rocks permitting entry into an unknown area and another department of the earth!

Immediately at this point, once again, the credibility of such a viewpoint appears very suspect. Things quickly become tentative and obscure, and all objectivity seems to disappear. No longer are the tribes traveling between the Black and Caspian Seas, or up through the plains of Russia, but their itinerary now suddenly takes on the character and appearance of science fiction.

Which is too bad! And yet that is probably the way it has to be! There is no easy method of describing the transition between where the tribes once were and where they now might be. To try to rationalize such a phenomenon is like trying to explain the Spirit World, what it is like and how it could be right here upon the earth. It is the same as talking about the people of Enoch, how an entire city was taken up and transported to some other place. The sum of it all is that these are just different kinds of subjects, and consequently they have to be considered within a very different context and set of circumstances.

No one will maybe ever come close to knowing where the lost tribes are unless he or she is willing to accept the possibility of some very unusual conditions. These very possibly include a transferal to a geographic location in another department of the earth. The circumstances suggest that after the highway, and the encounter with ice and rocks, there was the process of going from one type of existence into another--a passage, as it were, from things on the earth to things under the earth, or beneath. And if all of this is correct, none of it needs to be regarded as too unrealistic or hard to believe. Certainly it stays in line with general Christian practice and tradition.

It is also a concept that is supported in theory by an unusual and significant idea, which is that the earth is much more than just a geological entity. There are those who believe, for example, that this planet, in a very real sense, is alive and is going through some of the same stages as that of a human being. It had a birth, in other words, and someday it will die, after which there will be a type of resurrection. Also certain religious principles and ordinances are involved. The basis for these views, which are not held by people in general, is again found in modern scripture.

Moreover, it is the idea that a broadened concept of the earth, beyond that of pure geology, is more apt to accommodate the possibility of subterranean life. The earth is a versatile organism and is able to provide the necessary settings for any number of different kinds of events and phenomena. And if thinking people can allow for the microcosm of someone like Jonah surviving three days inside a whale, maybe they can then visualize the earth's capacity to sustain a macrocosm of a large nation of people somewhere beneath its surface!

Also this planet, by way of some kind of natural law, is said to be the site of the Spirit World which has a population of possibly more than seventy billion people. It should only be a logical step to the side, therefore, to say that in some way the earth is also providing a habitat for the lost tribes of Israel!

One thing is certain. The tribes once existed, and they did travel toward the land of the north. What they did when they arrived there is not clear, and there are very few clues to go by, but it does seem safe to say that eventually they reached a *rendezvous point*, a so-called *place of entry*, and from there went on to a final destination.

Before them was a new land, one where mankind had never been before. In addition, there was a new type of life that no one had ever experienced. And yet after the alleged encounter with ice and rock, the rest of their journey could have been a fairly normal occurrence.

Their route, like that of many other explorations in the world's history, might have followed a large river, or network of rivers, which in turn was only a small segment of a larger watercourse system. Theoretically, this was the gigantic water supply for the north countries, the place where huge floods both originate and subside. Another designation, of course, would be the fountains of waters or the fountains of the great deep.

And just as the tribes would go in by such a route, they could also later come out the same way. In fact, when the command is given someday for the waters to be gathered together again so that dry land can appear, a parallel meaning might well be intended: "Gather the waters together so that the ten tribes might appear!" And all of this could very well happen in a region somewhere beneath the surface of the earth!

A FINAL DESTINATION

References to things beneath the earth do not necessarily imply the conditions associated with a hollow earth theory. To say that science is wrong, for example, concerning the huge inner and outer cores that are supposed to exist at the earth's center is probably entirely unnecessary. Casually refuting the large amount of evidence which scientists have discovered through seismology and other methods is just not an educated thing to do. Besides, there are other possibilities as far as the ten tribes are concerned.

The important thing is to try to view the mysterious disappearance of the tribes in as logical a way as possible, keeping in mind the unusual circumstances involved. These could have included an itinerary of travel along a large river system for an untold number of miles, possibly resulting in a journey comparable to the year and a half spent in Arzareth. Environmental conditions at that time, as witnessed by an outside observer, might have been little different from those existing on the earth's surface. Without anyone knowing what was happening, however, the tribes theoretically followed a course which actually conveyed them to another department of the earth!

Again their destination would not have had to be deep in the earth's interior. Somewhere in the planet's mantle, at a reasonable distance below the crust, there could have been a suitable area which had been prepared for them. And in the same way that a population of 125 million is able to subsist on 146,000 square miles in present-day Japan, so a comparable number of people, according to unknown laws and principles, might very well be living on the same amount of territory in some other part of the earth's structure.

Although such a theory at first seems miraculous and unbelievable, the evidence does point in the direction of just such a place! First, it keeps the tribes in the right area of the globe, which is in the north countries. Second, it links their traveling and existence with the important aspect of water. Third, it utilizes the interaction of ice and rock in connection with a gateway or point of entrance.

Fourth, it gives meaning to the scriptures which refer to things under or beneath the earth. Fifth, it is part of a historical pattern or cycle in which the tribes possibly disappeared in much the same way that someday they will reappear. Sixth, the idea gains credibility from the parallel existence of both the City of Enoch and the Spirit World.

And finally, there is logic in the idea that the tribes had no other place to go! Since they were last known to be in the north countries traveling as a group and not merely diffusing among the nations, they either had to go up, so to speak, or to go down. To go up would be like the City of Enoch, an idea discounted because the two situations are so different. To go down, on the other hand, although unorthodox and revolutionary, appears to be a more logical solution, even though it raises some very serious questions.

One of the problems, of course, with any kind of hollow earth theory is that of postulating a feasible source of light and energy, an *internal sun*, as it were. Without this source, a large population of people probably would be unable to survive. Its absence would also interject a radically different kind of environment to which the ten tribes were unacclimated.

Miracles do happen, however, and alternative ways are usually found to accomplish things. One such example occurs in modern scripture.

When a people known as the Jaredites were themselves traveling in a distant land, they encountered the problem of providing some type of light source inside their barges. They had an ocean to cross, and they knew they would often be submerged in water. Their leader inquired of the Lord as to what should be done, and as things turned out, it was left up to the people to find their own solution.

The implication was that any number of solutions might have been used, all probably requiring some kind of divine intervention to make them work. It was also the idea that the people would first do their part, and the Lord would then take care of the rest.

In this particular instance, the solution consisted of sixteen stones, two for each barge, which the Lord illuminated by touching them with his finger. And although the stones evidently provided no energy source, they still gave much needed light for 344 days as the Jaredites crossed a large body of water, very possibly the Indian and Pacific Oceans.

What seems impossible for man is certainly not impossible for the Lord. If it is true that the ten tribes are currently living some kind of subterranean life, then the problem of providing light and energy will naturally be taken care of.

Many people, though, especially those in the scientific community, would maybe never accept this as a serious possibility. Nor would it be to their discredit, necessarily, not to do so. The use of intellect is very often separate from the exercise of faith, and unless a person is sensitive to both, he might neglect one principle in favor of the other.

The comment was once made that although a certain man was an intellectual giant, he was at the same time a spiritual pygmy. He knew many formulas and equations, but when it came to things pertaining to religion, he still had much to accomplish. The opposite might be true, of course, when someone focuses heavily on religion but has very little knowledge of science. What is too bad sometimes is that one group cannot be a little more tolerant and patient with the other.

Yet sooner or later, the truth is always discovered. "What is is, and what is not is not" is definitely a true statement, and also a standard of reality that governs the final outcome of things. There often has be a certain waiting period, however, in which opinions are explored and new ideas are tested. But truth does prevail, even though it might have been unpopular along the way.

In regard to the lost tribes of Israel, the main thing, once again, is to believe they exist and to try to visualize the actuality of their situation, whatever it happens to be. This is not always easy, and it has to be done sometimes when things are very vague and obscure.

It is interesting, for example, that such a dearth of information exists on this subject. Aside from a few scattered writings, along with the Apocrypha and some modern scripture, almost nothing is available on this lost civilization of people.

And yet they figure very prominently among many important things yet to come! During the time known as the end of the world, when the Lord returns and reigns personally upon the earth, miraculous events will occur, and some of these are directly related to the return of the ten lost tribes.

Jesus will stand upon the Mount of Olives at the end of the Battle of Armageddon and provide a release for those who are held captive in the city of Jerusalem. On that occasion the mount will cleave in two, one part going to the north and the other to the south, opening up a passageway through which the Jewish people can escape from their enemies.

At about the same time, the Lord will issue a final decree, commanding the waters of the great deep to return to the north countries. Accompanying this event will be dramatic upheavals of nature that will cause valleys to disappear and mountains to crumble. This also is the general time period in which the ten tribes finally will make their reappearance!

The tribes will come out of their hiding place in the north, ending a long season of isolation, and join with others who are of the House of Israel. They will be led by prophets who will smite the rocks and cause the ice to fall, permitting access to the outside world before them. After that, a highway will be cast up which will furnish a pathway across an expanse of water, possibly one pertaining to the Arctic Ocean or one of its adjacent seas!

THE EARTH AS A LIVING BEING

All of these things will take place in connection with the modern-day earth. They will be part of a grand culmination of events that began at least 6,000 years ago. Down through history, from the time of Adam and Eve to the present, from the early civilizations of Egypt and Mesopotamia to the technological nations of today, everything in a way has been just a prologue to the important events which are still to come.

And the setting for all this is the earth itself, a geological but living entity where much more exists than meets the eye. It involves a concept built upon the idea that this planet consists of more than core, mantle and crust, just as a human being is much more than heart, lungs, and a myriad of parts.

The earth, in fact, might be considered a living organism, even to the extent of possessing a soul. Just as the spirit and body constitute the soul of man, so might the combined spiritual and temporal parts of this planet be regarded as the soul of the earth. Such a concept emphasizes the earth's true identity and avoids the error of classing it merely as an astronomical or geologic sphere.

This means that the earth, following its birth or creation, eventually entered upon a course of mortal existence, including a type of probation. And during the last several thousand years, it has been going through certain stages that are comparable to those of a human being.

When Adam transgressed the law in the Garden of Eden, for example, it was not only he that fell but also the earth. The earth was cursed for Adam's sake and changed from an immortal to a mortal state. Like human beings, however, the

Figure 6

The Earth's Interior

From a scientific standpoint, the earth is composed of an inner and outer core, along with a mantle and crust. Data gained from modern seismology and other methods provide many clues as to what these areas are like.

At the same time, scriptural accounts suggest that the earth has an unusual potential and is possibly much more than what its geological features imply.

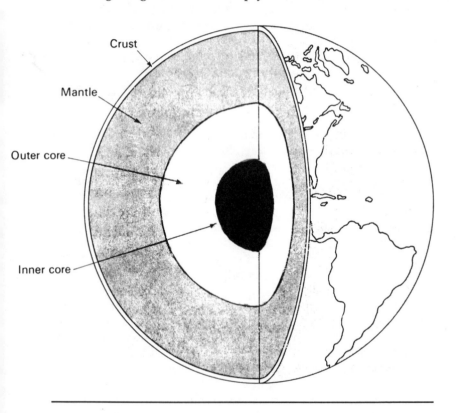

planet was not lost. Through the atonement of Jesus Christ, it was redeemed from the Fall and is now successfully filling the measure of its creation. According to modern scripture, it is currently abiding the law of the Celestial Kingdom and will one day become the abode of celestial beings.

In the meantime, the earth is subject to the basic religious ordinances of being born of the water and of the Spirit. Its baptism by water occurred during the time of the great Flood, and the baptism of Spirit, and also by fire, will take place at the end of the world just prior to the Millennium. It is then that the earth will be renewed and restored to its former glory.

After that will come another thousand years of history, following which the earth will eventually die and then be quickened or resurrected. This will complete the process that must be accomplished in order for it to obtain its own salvation and exaltation.

Such an unusual view of the earth, once more, is the result of modern scripture. It is both unorthodox and revolutionary, and consequently there are many people who maybe will not accept it. If it is true, however, it not only portrays a new concept of the earth but also forms an additional basis for the reality and existence of the lost tribes of Israel!

It is also one of those aspects of human experience that involves the exercise of faith as well as the use of intellect, especially in regard to the earth having a soul. In connection with this, the following scripture provides a good example.

"And it came to pass that Enoch looked upon the earth; and he heard a voice from the bowels thereof, saying: Wo, wo is me, the mother of men. I am pained, I am weary, because of the wickedness of my children. When shall I rest, and be cleansed from the filthiness which is gone forth out of me? When will my Creator sanctify me, that I may rest, and righteousness for a season abide upon my face?" [23]

Of course, this account could be interpreted only as a literary device, the personification of an inanimate object in order to convey a certain effect or idea. And yet possibly there is another meaning, which is that the earth has a spiritual purpose, in addition to one that is physical, and is playing a very unique role in the universe.

Whatever the earth's status, therefore, whether a living entity with unusual characteristics or just another planet revolving around the sun, one thing seems apparent, and that is that there are certain factors involved that generally have gone undetected and unexplored. It suggests that some things pertaining to the structure of the earth are still very much unknown. At least the implications are there.

And as far as the ten tribes are concerned, their existence in some kind of subterranean locality does not appear now to be entirely out of the question. Such a view is not the easiest to visualize or promote, yet it is not completely untenable either. It merely accepts the possibility that the earth has an unusual potential, one which could maybe explain the whereabouts of a missing group of people.

Finally, all of this might gain some additional credibility by way of the sign of Jonas. This was used by Jesus at one time when people asked for a special proof of his divinity. There would be no sign given, he told them, except one they had already received, which was the sign of Jonas. "For as Jonas was three days and three nights in the whale's belly, so shall the Son of Man be three days and three nights in the heart of the earth." [24] This is all he would tell them.

There are two things about this last scripture that make it relevant and interesting. First is the credibility aspect. If someone can accept the account of Jonah and the whale, and from there go on to the reality of the resurrection, it might then become a logical third step to consider the possibility of some kind of subterranean life for the ten tribes.

Second is the reference to "the heart of the earth," an area synonymous with the world of spirits. This was the place that Jesus visited as his body lay in the garden tomb, and while there, according to the Bible, he preached to the spirits in prison. The circumstances pertaining to this particular area, however, are still extremely vague, as is the locality of the heart of the earth.

Does the Spirit World, for example, refer to a region above the earth or beneath? And what about the heart of the earth? Could this have any kind of relevance or similarity to where the lost tribes are presently located? Regardless of any answers that might be given, such questions continue to be a provocative subject and an important matter of interest.

And so do the tribes themselves! Right from the beginning, when they broke away from their original group, they became a distinct and unusual people headed in a new direction. The way they got their start, and the manner in which their leader was chosen, both suggest that they had a different kind of destiny. And whereas they had once been in a household of twelve tribes, linked together by a common heritage and tradition, they now found themselves alone, and their number was suddenly reduced to ten!

THE COMPOSITION OF THE TRIBES

Although it is customary to refer to the lost tribes of Israel as being ten in number, originally they were more like eleven and a half. As things turned out, however, certain changes occurred, and when the time arrived for them to migrate into the north country, they were probably very close to their traditional number.

In the beginning, just before Solomon's kingdom split in two, the genesis of the ten tribes was foretold by Ahijah the prophet. Ahijah took a man named Jeroboam to the side one day and informed him that he was to be the king of the future Kingdom of Israel. Solomon's son Rehoboam, in turn, would become the leader of the Kingdom of Judah.

To illustrate and dramatize this coming event, the prophet took from Jeroboam a brand new coat he was wearing and ripped it into twelve pieces, ten of which he handed back to its owner. "Take thee ten pieces," he said, "for thus saith the Lord, the God of Israel, Behold, I will rend the kingdom out of the hand of Solomon and will give ten tribes to thee."

He also told him that none of this would take place until after Solomon died. "But I will take the kingdom out of his son's hand," the Lord said, "and will give it unto thee, even ten tribes. And unto his son will I give one tribe, that David my servant may have a light alway before me in Jerusalem, the city which I have chosen me to put my name there." [25]

In round numbers, therefore, there were to be ten tribes for Jeroboam and one tribe for Rehoboam, although in actuality it was more like eleven and a half to one king and one and a half to the other. The tribes constituting the Kingdom of Israel consisted of (1) Reuben, (2) Simeon, (3) Dan, (4) Naphtali, (5) Gad, (6) Asher, (7) Issachar, (8) Zebulun, (9) Ephraim and (10) Manasseh, plus the tribe of Levi and also part of the tribe of

Benjamin. This left the other kingdom with its main tribe of Judah along with the remaining part of Benjamin.

At different places in the biblical record, it states that only a single tribe was to be in the Kingdom of Judah. Yet as Rehoboam prepared to go to battle in an attempt to keep Judah and Israel together, he assembled an army of 180,000 men, not just from the tribe of Judah but also from Benjamin whose geographical area was immediately to the north. An account of this event, along with others in the Bible, reaffirms the fact that Judah and at least part of Benjamin were both on the side of Rehoboam.

Originally the tribe of Levi was included with Jeroboam's new kingdom, and although the Levites, because of their special religious calling, had no geographical inheritance in Palestine like that of the other tribes, they still represented a sizable population of people.

It was not their lot, however, to stay with the Kingdom of Israel. Jeroboam's religious innovations and idolatrous practices eventually became so bad that the Levites transferred to the other kingdom. Actually they were cast out by Jeroboam who replaced them with a new priesthood of his own.

This left the Kingdom of Judah, whose capital was at Jerusalem, with the tribes of Judah and Levi, along with the part pertaining to Benjamin. In addition, there might also have been a certain percentage of the adjoining tribe of Dan, as well as small groups from the other tribes whose religious feelings inclined them more toward the southern kingdom than the north.

The Kingdom of Israel, therefore, with capitals first at Shechem and Tirzah, and later in nearby Samaria, contained the remaining part of the tribes. Nineteen kings guided the affairs of this large group of people for more than 200 years, right up until the time that their nation was finally conquered by the invading forces of the Assyrian Empire!

Figure 7

The Division of Tribes

Kingdom of Israel

1. Reuben
2. Simeon
3. Levi
4. Dan
5. Naphtali
6. Gad
7. Ashur
8. Issachar
9. Zebulun
10. Ephraim
11. Manasseh
12. Benjamin (part)

Kingdom of Judah

1. Judah
2. Benjamin (part)
3. Others

Soon after the division of the House of Israel during the 10th Century B.C., the Levites transferred over to the Kingdom of Judah in the south. (II Chronicles 11:13-14)

A scattering of people from various other tribes, who preferred living in Judah and Jerusalem, also became part of the southern kingdom.

ASSYRIAN CAPTIVITY

From the very start, when Jeroboam took over as the new king of Israel, the nation began a long spiral downward. The king instituted reforms that he thought would fortify his position, but at the same time planted the seeds for future destruction.

Because of this, it was made known unto him what eventually would happen. Ahijah, the same prophet who earlier had informed Jeroboam of his coming kingship, now prophesied of less fortunate things to come, including the conquest of the ten tribes and their consignment to Assyrian captivity.

"For the Lord shall smite Israel," he said, "as a reed is shaken in the water, and he shall root up Israel out of this good land, which he gave to their fathers, and shall scatter them beyond the river, because they have made their groves, provoking the Lord to anger." [26]

It was a dire forecast, one that evidently did not impress Jeroboam at the time, but after more than two centuries, everything took place as predicted. Invading forces from the north, coming out of the Assyrian Empire, struck quickly at the wayward kingdom, disrupting the population and carrying many of the people captive. Foreigners were brought in from the outside to occupy the land. And when the capital city of Samaria was finally taken, Israel ceased to exist as a nation!

Assyria's conquest of the Kingdom of Israel at this time consisted mainly of two phases. The first was the subjugation of Transjordan and northern Palestine by Tiglath-Pileser III in about 733 B.C. in which the country was annexed to the Assyrian Empire and part of its population deported to foreign cities in the north. This occurred while Pekah was the Israelite ruler.

Pekah and his forces had earlier gone to war against neighboring Judah, killing 120,000 people in one day, according to the Bible, and taking 200,000 men, women and children captive. In a way, it was a preview of what later happened to Israel at the hands of the Asssyrians.

"In the days of Pekah, king of Israel, came Tiglath-Pileser, king of Assyria, and took Ijon, and Abelbethmaachah, and Janoah, and Kedesh, and Hazor, and Gilead, and Galilee, all the land of Naphtali, and carried them captive to Assyria."

"And he carried them away, even the Reubenites, and the Gadites, and half the tribe of Manasseh, and brought them unto Halah, and Habor, and Hara, and to the river Gozan, unto this day." [27]

Besides the tribes of Reuben, Gad, and part of Manasseh, these conquered regions also contained people from the tribes of Asher, Zebulun, Naphtali, Issachar and Dan.

It was Assyrian policy during this time period not to deport the entire population of an area but only about one-half. Then by bringing in colonists from other parts of the empire to take their place, the new rulers weakened the existing social structure and were able to maintain a stronger control. [28]

Also the people that were actually deported appear to have been mostly from the upper classes, including political and ecclesiastical leaders, artisans, and those from the aristocracy. Anyone who was from the lower classes, therefore, was more apt to be left behind.

Such a policy constituted an important factor in the early conquest of the ten tribes. Many of the people were taken away as prisoners, but there were others who remained and intermingled with the incoming colonists, eventually turning into a hybrid group. All of this undoubtedly devastated the

Figure 8

Two Phases of Assyrian Conquest

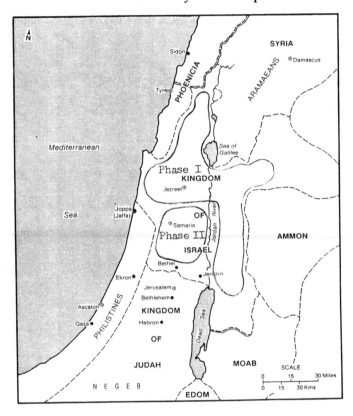

In the first phase of Assyrian invasions, occurring about 733 B.C., Tiglath-Pileser III conquered the tribes living in northern Palestine and Transjordan. The second phase took place during approximately 724 to 721 B.C. when the capital city of Samaria fell. This invasion was begun by Shalmaneser V and evidently concluded by his successor Sargon II.

The people taken captive into Assyria during these conquests were later referred to as the ten lost tribes of Israel.

Figure 9

Tiglath-Pileser III*

The Assyrian king who commenced the invasion of the ten tribes was Tiglath-Pileser III. He is first mentioned in the Bible as *Pul*. Originally, he left the Israelites alone as long as they would pay tribute but later led his forces into Transjordan and northern Palestine, annexing the territory to the Assyrian Empire and taking many prisoners.

*Andre Parrot, *Samaria, the Capital of the Kingdom of Israel* (New York: Philosophical Library, Incorporated, 1958), p. 47.

country, and what was even worse, there was another invasion still to come.

The second phase of Assyrian captivity, which occurred during the reign of Hoshea, was the conquest of the capital city of Samaria, along with related territory in the north and to the south. These areas generally included the tribes of Ephraim and Simeon, and also parts of Benjamin and Manasseh. The Assyrian army was now led by Shalmaneser V who commenced the invasion in approximately 724 B.C.

"Then the king of Assyria came up throughout all the land and went up to Samaria and besieged it three years. In the ninth year of Hoshea, the king of Assyria took Samaria, and carried Israel away into Assyria, and placed them in Halah and in Habor by the river Gozan, and in the cities of the Medes." [29]

The embattled kingdom actually held out longer than might have been expected, and it was in about 721 B.C. when the end finally occurred. By that time Assyria had a new king named Sargon II, and on his way home from a campaign in Egypt some two years later, he stopped in Israel and took 27,290 people captive, deporting them in the usual manner to different parts of the Assyrian Empire. [30]

In one of his inscriptions which commemorated this event, Sargon wrote the following: "The man of Samaria and a king who was hostile to me had joined together to refuse homage and tribute to me, and came out to fight with me. By the help of the great gods, my lords, I overthrew them: I captured from them 27,280 persons with their chariots, their gods in whom they trusted, and took as my royal share of the booty 200 chariots. I gave orders that the rest should be settled in the midst of Assyria." [31]

Again the prisoners taken were evidently from the upper classes--the intelligentsia, so to speak, that the Assyrians were mostly thinking about as far as trouble and insurrection were concerned. And like the others before them, the tribes were carried captive into Assyria, and new colonists brought in to take their place.

Figure 10

Sargon II*

Of the three Assyrian rulers who were involved in the conquest of the ten tribes, Sargon II was probably the most well-known. He appears to have been king when Samaria, the capital of the Kingdom of Israel, fell to invaders. And although he might not have been present at the time, he evidently was the one who later took more than 27,000 people captive.

*Andre Parrot, *Samaria, the Capital of the Kingdom of Israel* (New York: Philosophical Library, Incorporated, 1958), p. 50.

"So was Israel carried away out of their own land to Assyria unto this day. And the King of Assyria brought men from Babylon, and from Cuthah, and from Ava, and from Hamath, and from Sepharvaim, and placed them in the cities of Samaria instead of the children of Israel: and they possessed Samaria and dwelt in the cities thereof." [32]

The northern area where all of the tribes were deported was mainly between the upper reaches of the Tigris and Euphrates Rivers, not too far from the city of Nineveh. Other captivity sites might have been farther to the east, although how far from the center of the empire is uncertain. The only clue is that one of the regions is referred to as the cities of the Medes.

This was the locality, therefore, where the ten tribes spent the years of their captivity, a period of time generally undetected in Israelite history. Unlike the exiles from Judah who were later taken captive into Babylonia, an account of the tribes during their stay in Assyria is almost completely unknown. For many years, however, possibly a century or more, they were prisoners in a foreign land, fulfilling all the predictions which had been made by the prophets.

But it was not always to be that way. The political situation changed, and a people known as the Chaldeans eventually took over in Mesopotamia. No longer was Assyria the dominant power. Their dreaded rule finally came to an end, and a new period of history began, all of which might partially explain why the tribes were suddenly able to turn their backs on the ruling powers and walk away.

And yet the time had definitely arrived for them to make their move! It was the Lord who was setting the timetable, and the hour had now come for a long journey northward to begin!

It was people from all of the ten tribes who were going, but not all of those who originally were in those tribes. Many were being left behind in Palestine and Transjordan to mix with incoming colonists.

Figure 11

Assyrian Captivity Sites

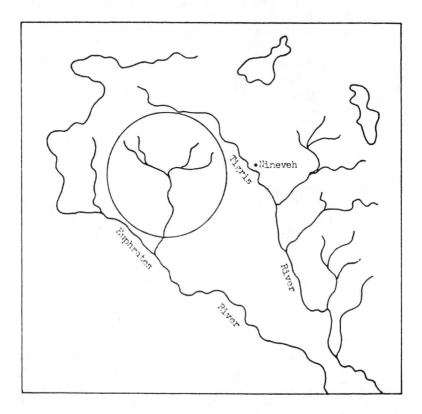

The main areas of captivity were in cities called Halah, Habor and Hara, located in upper Mesopotamia between the Tigris and Euphrates Rivers. Other sites might have been farther to the east in a region which the Bible refers to as the cities of the Medes.

In Samaria, for example, a foreign population joined together with the remaining Israelites, creating a group later known as the Samaritans. It was these people during the time of Jesus that the Jews held so much in derision and disrespect. They looked down on them as an inferior breed, hybrids as it were, whose ancestry was not pure Israelite but a mix with implantations from the north.

In contrast with this, the migrating tribes constituted a much more controlled lineage of people, especially when they stayed separate as a group during their captivity. Not only did they maintain a distinct identity as children of Israel, but since they were generally from the upper classes, they probably possessed more culture and education.

None of this seemed to matter to Jesus, however, during his ministry in Palestine. In fact, there were times when he cited the Samaritans as models for the Jews to follow. It was a member of this group, for example, that stopped to help the injured man on the road to Jericho. Another was the only one among ten lepers who, upon being miraculously healed, remembered to turn back and thank the Lord. Also it was the woman at the well in Samaria who showed so much interest and respect for Jesus and his teachings and accepted him as the Messiah.

Yet an important point does exist. And that is that the tribes who made their way north were marked for a strange and unusual destiny, one that required the attributes of a good stock of people. It is not that they were better than those who were left behind, in opposition to some of the teachings of Jesus, but they at least had the potential of perpetuating a sturdy race and a strong civilization. They were the cream of the crop, so to speak, and also the flower of the nation.

This was an important factor during the centuries that followed as the tribes settled in a new area and took over the land which had been prepared for them!

JESUS AND THE LOST TRIBES

One of the main things Jesus did following his death and resurrection, according to modern scripture, was to visit two other groups of people, first those known as the Nephites, and then sometime later the lost tribes of Israel. Both of these were part of the *other sheep* he had spoken of earlier in Palestine.

"And other sheep I have," he said, "which are not of this fold: them also I must bring, and they shall hear my voice; and there shall be one fold and one shepherd." [33]

When he visited the Nephites, a civilization living on the American Continent, he told them that they were some of the people he had been talking about. But there were still others, he said, those who were not of ancient America, nor of the land of Jerusalem, or any other place where he had been to minister. There were also the ten lost tribes!

"But now I go unto the Father," he told them, "and also to show myself unto the lost tribes of Israel, for they are not lost unto the Father, for he knoweth whither he hath taken them." [34]

Jesus stated several times that the tribes were at a separate location and had been led away and taken there by his Father. No one knew where they were, he said, and he had been commanded not to reveal their whereabouts.

He also told the Nephites that in the latter days a marvelous work would occur throughout the world, and that the remnants of the House of Israel which were scattered across the earth would be gathered. "Verily, I say unto you," he said, "at that day shall the work of the Father commence among all the dispersed of my people, yea, even the tribes which have been lost, which the Father hath led away out of Jerusulem."

"Yea, and then shall the work commence, with the Father, among all nations, in preparing the way whereby his people may be gathered home to the land of their inheritance." [35]

One of the events of this latter-day gathering, according to early Nephite records, was to be an accumulation of all religious scripture written by different groups of people down through history. "For behold, I shall speak unto the Jews and they shall write it," the Lord said, "and I shall also speak unto the Nephites and they shall write it; and I shall also speak unto the other tribes of the house of Israel, which I have led away, and they shall write it."

"And it shall come to pass that the Jews shall have the words of the Nephites, and the Nephites shall have the words of the Jews; and the Nephites and the Jews shall have the words of the lost tribes of Israel; and the lost tribes of Israel shall have the words of the Nephites and the Jews." [36]

The sharing of written scripture, therefore, was to play an important part in the events pertaining to the last days. And this will be particularly significant in regard to the ten lost tribes.

When the tribes return out of the north countries, at a time when the waters of the great deep are driven back to their source and the earth is restored to the way it was before the days of Peleg, they will be led by prophets and will carry with them a certain treasure of great value to their civilization. Their pathway will be laid before them, as in olden times, and the Spirit of the Almighty will be their shield and their protection.

"And they shall bring forth their rich treasures," the Lord has said, "unto the children of Ephraim, my servants. And the boundaries of the everlasting hills shall tremble at their presence." [37]

The rich treasures of the lost tribes might refer to any number of things, of course, but one of them could certainly be their literary heritage, including written scripture, historical records, general literature and genealogy. All of these would be valuable sources of information, especially the scripture, as well as an important key to unlocking the mystery which for so long has surrounded this amazing group of people!

JOURNEY TOWARD THE POLE

In their journey to the north following the Assyrian captivity, the ten tribes covered an undetermined amount of territory and, according to the apocryphal record, spent the last year and a half traveling through a country called Arzareth. Their route, which is only a matter of speculation, always pointed in the same general direction and possibly took them along the eastern coast of the Black Sea.

From there, if they continued straight northward, they would have traveled through Russia and eventually across the Barents Sea to a large group of islands known as Franz Josef Land. And after that, there was the Arctic Ocean and the North Pole. Most of this region beyond the mainland was a vast wilderness, a desolate area of ice and snow.

Whether or not the tribes exceeded the limits of continental Asia, however, entering the frozen regions farther north, is again merely conjecture, but if they did, there is no better way of approximating the conditions of their journey than to compare them with Robert E. Peary's expedition to the North Pole in the winter and spring of 1909.

This expedition, like several others that preceded it, took Peary and his group into a huge wasteland. After leaving their land station at Cape Columbia near the northern coast of Greenland, they headed north across the polar sea, threading their way through a long series of ice floes, pressure ridges, and leads, or open water.

It was the ice, by far, that was the most dominant part of the landscape. It was everywhere in all kinds of conditions, shapes and sizes. Always present in the daytime, and at night grinding and groaning in the distance, it spread like a huge blanket in all directions. At least nine-tenths of the country

Figure 12

The Travel Route

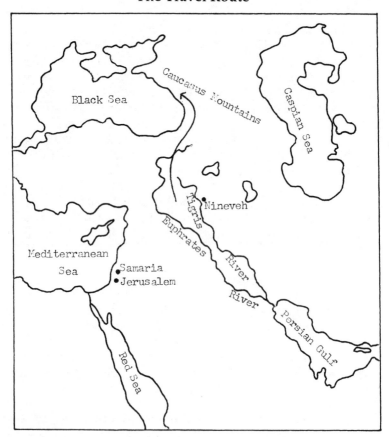

From their captivity sites in upper Mesopotamia, the tribes started their journey northward. According to the Apocrypha, which is still a questionable source of information, they first crossed the Euphrates River, and then after that, a logical route would have been to the left of the Caucasus Mountains and along the eastern coast of the Black Sea.

---

which the party traversed consisted of ice floes--the large, rough masses covering the surface of the Arctic Ocean.

But it was the leads, the treacherous spaces of open water, that presented the challenges, and also the most serious problems. During one of Peary's expeditions, for example, he and his group almost lost their lives when a large lead opened up in front of them, temporarily cutting off their return to the mainland. In the final expedition in 1909, one of the explorers drowned in this same region.

The leads varied in size anywhere from small cracks to large lakes or rivers, one-half mile to two miles across and farther than the eye could see to the right or left. They were always a matter of concern, and a continual source of trouble and danger.

According to Peary, such leads were "the ever-present nightmare of the traveler over the frozen surface of the polar ocean." Their occurrence or nonoccurrence was a thing impossible to predict or calculate. "They open without warning immediately ahead of the traveler," he said, "following no apparent rule or law of action. They are the unknown quantity of the polar equation." [38]

It was ice, water and snow, therefore, that were the main features of the north country, and yet two other conditions-- the wind and low temperatures--were also crucial factors. The wind became so strong sometimes that it had the impact of a wall of water, and the intensely cold weather could drop to as low as sixty degrees below zero. Both of these played a significant part in Peary's expedition.

Between Cape Columbia and the North Pole, a distance of more than 400 miles, one thing was noticeably missing, however, and that was land. There also were no colors, to speak of--only the continual white of ice and snow, along with dark clouds which often formed over the stretches of dark water.

And yet back on the mainland, landforms were always a prominent feature, blending in contrast with the enveloping whiteness. Some of these areas made very picturesque scenes, and one of them along the coasts of Greenland prompted Peary at one time to record the following comment.

"There is a crystalline clearness in the pure atmosphere," he said, "that gives to all colors a brilliancy seen nowhere else--the glittering white of the icebergs with the blue veins running through them; the deep reds, warm grays, and rich browns of the cliffs, streaked here and there with the yellows of the sandstone; a little farther away sometimes the soft green grass of this little arctic oasis; and on the distant horizon the steel blue of the great inland ice." [39]

In connection with Peary's expedition, this kind of scene is one that also brings to mind another picture, an imaginary view of the ten tribes, for example, when they eventually arrived at their preliminary destination. At an unknown location, whether in the vicinity of the mainland or on some island, they made the transfer from one geographical area to another, first along a possible highway that allowed passage over an expanse of water, and then through some kind of opening in the ice and rock.

This last stage of events was their embarkation point, the northern gateway and place of entry. And in that setting, far from their distant homeland, they mysteriously and miraculously disappeared in the north country!

Yet when all of this took place, if it actually did, it might never have occurred in a region so far to the north. Although ice possibly played an important part in the disappearance of the ten tribes, as it definitely will do in the future when they return, it does not necessarily imply a gateway place reaching extensively into the arctic and polar regions. To promote this idea as a possibility might be extending the location too far north, especially in view of the severe environmental conditions around the Arctic Ocean.

Even though the North Pole Expedition of 1909 was well equipped with both men and supplies, Peary himself admitted that they never could have made it without the Eskimos and the dogs that pulled the sledges. These two resources especially, native to the land which outsiders were trying to conquer, were the two main things that made the difference.

The point is that the tribes were from an area in and around Mesopotamia, and to project them extremely far into the north country could be putting them beyond a reasonable capability to survive. In the vicinity of northern Russia, either on the mainland or on some island, there are innumerable places that could satisfy the requirements of ice, rock, and water without going farther north.

Once again, much of this is only conjecture and speculation, but at the same time also an attempt to reinforce the reality and existence of the ten lost tribes.

THE LAST GREAT EVENT

In a final analysis, and after all that has been said about this extraordinary group of people, it is again not so much a question as to where they are that is important, or under what conditions they might be living, but rather the acceptance of the fact that they do actually exist. At this moment in time, in the closing years of the twentieth century, they are definitely residing somewhere, awaiting the signal that will once more start them moving toward a new land and in a new direction.

To believe in such an occurrence, and to anticipate it, is an integral part of a great latter-day movement. Along with other momentous events, such as the establishment of Zion, the rebuilding of the temple in Jerusalem, the Battle of Armageddon, and the final gathering of waters, it will be in company with the grand preliminary to the second coming of Jesus Christ. Then the earth will know the truthfulness of all these things.

The return of the tribes especially will emphasize the importance of this dramatic period in history. Their reappearance will symbolize the gathering of all the House of Israel and the restoration of everything to the way it was in the beginning. And as far as the tribes themselves are concerned, it will be a time when they finally realize a spiritual fulfillment which has been denied them all down through the centuries.

Just as a group of people in some isolated part of Russia, Africa, or China might anticipate the visit to a holy shrine or temple, so the lost tribes of Israel, after these many years, will have the opportunity of traveling to Zion and receiving the award that awaits them. "And there shall they fall down and be crowned with glory, even in Zion, by the hands of the servants of the Lord, even the children of Ephraim." [40]

In that day it will be Ephraim, in a sense, receiving blessings from Ephraim, two groups of Israelites, both descended from the same progenitor and one group being acknowledged by the other. One will be the recipient of an important religious endowment, and the other the benefactor. It will be Ephraim of old being blessed by a kindred group who likewise stems from Ephraim, or who has become a member of that lineage through adoption.

During pre-captivity days, the Kingdom of Israel was sometimes referred to as Ephraim, as well as Israel, especially by the prophet Hosea. [41] This was partly because Ephraim was the most prominent tribe and often asserted itself beyond the authority of the others. Also the first person known by that name had received a special birthright among all twelve of the tribes, even though he was a junior member, and this important status had a determining influence among the Israelites in general.

The tribe of Ephraim, therefore, was of particular importance and consequently possessed a very unusual destiny. Not only did part of it join the ten tribes who went into the north country, but others stayed behind--some who possibly broke off from the migrating group, and also those who originally remained in Palestine. Aside from the tribes who were lost, therefore, the seed of Ephraim was dispersed among the nations, later to appear in an important latter-day role.

In any case, the tribe of Ephraim from the very beginning appears to have been a preeminent group, one marked for leadership and responsibility. Joshua, the successor to Moses, was himself an Ephraimite. This preeminence continued as an important factor among the ten tribes during much of their history, and when the time comes for those who were lost to reappear, it will maybe be Ephraim once again that will lead them!

Wherever the tribes are at present, there are prophets among them, or at least there have been from time to time. It has also been said that the Apostle John, the close disciple of Jesus and one who was not to taste of death until the Lord's second coming, has been among these people at one time or another, preparing them for their future return.

All of these things again point toward a time, maybe not too far away, when remarkable and unusual events are scheduled to occur. And not the least among these will be when Ephraim of old comes out of the north to be crowned in glory by another Ephraim in the south, joining together two important branches of the House of Israel.

The earth will be a much different place in those days. America, for example, will be entering a new period of history, having gone through many revolutions and natural disasters. The entire face of the land will be altered, and vast changes will take place. Some of these future events, one of which pertains to the ten tribes, were predicted by Joseph Smith, the Mormon prophet, in a letter to an editor in 1833.

"And now I am prepared to say by the authority of Jesus Christ," he said, "that not many years shall pass away before the United States shall present such a scene of bloodshed as has not a parallel in the history of our nation. Pestilence, hail, famine, and earthquake will sweep the wicked of this generation from off the face of the land, to open and prepare the way for the return of the lost tribes of Israel from the north country." [42]

The destination of the tribes as they journey toward the south will be the heart of America, close to the geographical center in an area of western Missouri. This is the place designated for a future city to be known as Zion, or the New Jerusalem, and it is here that the scheduled rendezvous of the two Ephraims will occur.

Zion will also be the scene of many other important events. As one of two world capitals in the future, the other being in Jerusalem, it will be the principal focal point upon the American Continent, serving as a hub for all religious, political, economic and social activity. In every aspect of human life, it will be the epitome of everything that is perfect

Figure 13

A Place of Entry and a Place of Exit

An interesting observation is that the ten tribes possibly approached the north country starting at about 42 degrees east longitude, passing along the eastern coast of the Black Sea. But in the last days, they might be coming down from the north on the opposite side of the globe toward a site in what is now western Missouri, about 94 degrees west longitude. This suggests a place of exit different from the original place of entry, although not necessarily.

---

and true. And the main authority in this city, as well as in areas surrounding it, will be the Lord Jesus Christ!

"And he shall utter his voice out of Zion, and he shall speak from Jerusalem, and his voice shall be heard among all people." "And the land of Jerusalem and the land of Zion shall be turned back into their own place, and the earth shall be like as it was in the days before it was divided. And the Lord, even the Savior, shall stand in the midst of his people, and shall reign over all flesh." [43]

At one time during the latter days, the Lord will also stand upon Mount Zion, or in the New Jerusalem, and with him will be 144,000 ministers of the gospel. This large assembly will comprise 12,000 men from each of the twelve tribes except Dan and will be part of a huge missionary effort before the end of the world. The lost tribes will possibly figure very prominently in this last great crusade, an event closely associated with the gathering of the House of Israel.

Exactly when all of this will happen, along with other predicted events, is not always clear. But even when chronology is questionable, the important thing is that sooner or later everything will eventually take place.

Also one thing of significance is that so many outstanding events will be occurring at about the same time, either just before, during, or right after the second coming of Christ. Among these will be a gathering of the waters, the third and final time when a flood recedes and causes millions of square miles of dry land to appear!

Again the chronology is uncertain, but sometime in the vicinity of the Lord's second advent, he will issue the command for the waters of the great deep to be driven back into the north countries. Somewhere, and in some way, a tremendous volume of ocean will be absorbed or redistributed, and the earth's surface again will become like it was in the beginning. The land will appear much like it did following the Creation and during the time of Noah, and possibly also after the great Flood before the days of Peleg. At that time, according to religious prophecies, there will be one continuous length of land forming a belt around much of the earth. A sea will still exist, and areas of open water, but a great deal less than at present.

Whatever the land surface of the world looked like several thousand years ago, previous to the Flood and before the division of the earth, that is the way it will look again after the final gathering of waters. All things will be changed back to a paradisiacal state. Geographical conditions will be much different then, and the capitals of Zion and Jerusalem will both be on the same continent.

And so it will be that in the last days, great and marvelous events will occur, each at the right time and in the right order. Nothing will be left to chance. Everything that has been foretold in scripture will take place, and all the words of the prophets will be fulfilled.

These final occurrences, once again, will include not only the last gathering of the waters but also the restoration of the ten tribes. Both of these, engulfed for so long in an aura of mystery, will be instrumental in ushering in a new period of the world's history. In addition, each will commence in response to a divine command.

"Gather the waters together and cause the dry land to appear!" Twice down through the centuries these words have rung out like a war cry, heralding a new age and a new beginning. They occurred at the time of Creation and were implied at the close of the great Flood, and once again in the future they will be part of a divine decree that will drive the seas and oceans back into the north country!

At about this same time, when another signal is given, the ten lost tribes will begin their long journey homeward, coming out of concealment and pointing southward toward the place called Zion. There in a new land and in a brand new city, they will fall down before their kinsmen of old and be crowned with glory, after which a new era in the long history of the House of Israel will then begin!

Figure 14

Different Faces of the Earth

In the beginning of the world's recorded history, following the Creation, the surface of the earth was much different from what it is today. Scriptural evidence indicates a greater amount of land at that time in proportion to water, with all of the land joined together in one area. The diagram below suggests one of the possibilities.

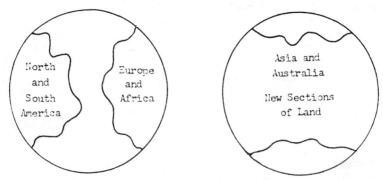

At the time of the great Flood, of course, the situation changed dramatically, as it did also possibly during the days of Peleg. In the first instance, the globe was partially or completely inundated by water, and in the second, major portions of land once more disappeared as the result of a third flood.

Geography since that time has remained basically the same. Yet according to religious prophecy, everything will someday return to a previous condition, and the amount of land will again greatly increase. The earth will then be renewed and receive a paradisiacal glory.

Figure 15

A View of Pangaea*

According to Alfred Wegener, the well-known proponent of continental drift, this is possibly what the earth looked like before the continents started drifting apart. He referred to the original area as *Pangaea*.

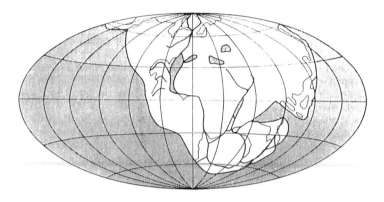

The concept of Pangaea is a reminder that someday in the future the earth allegedly will be restored to the way it was several thousand years ago. During that former time period, due to a large runoff of water, the landmass was much more extensive than it is today and was generally located together in one place. This condition, however, is not to be confused with Pangaea itself, which is said to have existed over 200 million years earlier.

*A. Hallum, *A Revolution in the Earth Sciences* (Oxford: Clarendon Press, 1973), p. 11.

POETRY

The poem which follows is a fictional account of the lost tribes of Israel responding to the call of modern-day prophets and coming out of their homeland.

EXODUS VII
by Clay McConkie

Without looking back
I walked over the last remaining hills
And left the valley behind me,

The valley where I was born,
And grew up,
And where I had raised a family.

During the time of the great waters,
I left the only place I had ever known
And headed north beyond the lowland
And along the foot of the tall mountains.

I was not the only one.
There were others going with me,
Those who were also leaving the valley
For the last time,

And we, in turn,
Would someday reach a rendezvous place
And join with thousands more
Who, like us, were on their long journey
Toward the north.

Mainly we followed the river,
Channeled off to the side in the canyons
     below us,
The wild tempestuous river
Whose waters, now at flood stage,
Were coming down from the mountains.

It was the river
That would be our compass and guide
In the days ahead,
Just as it had been the signal
To leave our homes in the valley
And find a new place to live.

For a long time now
Water had been coming from the north,
Filling lakes and reservoirs
In the valleys below.

And farther down,
The great sea was also rising,
Its waters always encroaching
Upon the mainland.

It was a crucial time,
The time of the great waters,
Nature's way, perhaps, of saying
That everyone should leave.

And yet another signal had also been
     given.
The Lord had spoken,
And the prophets had heard his voice,
And their words quickly went out
Among the people,
Proclaiming that the hour had finally
     arrived
For the long journey to begin.

The ancient prophecies
Were all fulfilled, they said,
And now was the time
To strike out across the mountains.

But it was a troubled time
And many refused to leave,
My own family being among them.
Many ignored the voice of the prophets
And denied the reality
Of any kind of divine message
Or any danger of an approaching flood.

As for me,
I had always put my faith
In the prophets.
I had also read the signs in the valley
Which were there for all to see,

The long terraces along the mountainside
And the prehistoric shorelines
Of an ancient ocean,
Confirmation that all the valleys and hills
Had once been covered with water.
And I knew the same thing
was happening again!

There were also the ancient traditions
        of my fathers,
The stories of Abraham and Jacob
And the ten tribes of Israel.
These were my people and my heritage.
I knew it, and I could not deny it!

And when the prophets said
It was time to leave,
I told them I was ready to go,
Even though it meant leaving my family.

Such were my thoughts
As I walked up through the mountains,
High above the raging river,
And they caused me to stop for a moment
And finally look back
Toward the country far below.

The view of the valley was gone now,
Yet I knew where it was.
Also I knew what would happen soon,
And I felt a deep remorse
For all those who were being left behind.

✳ ✳ ✳

As we dropped down into another valley
Several months later
Into the place of rendezvous,
We joined with many others
And then waited for those who were still
      to come.

In this modern camp of Israel
We mingled with people
Who were of the same mind and the same
      heart
And who had all things in common,

Who believed the ancient and modern
      scriptures
And the old traditions of the fathers,
And who also had committed themselves
      to forsake all
And follow the living prophets.

These were modern Israel's ten tribes
Whose ancestors many centuries before
Had come into the valleys of the mountains
To find refuge from an outside world
And to start a new life and a new beginning.

These also were the progeny
Of ancient tribesmen,
From Reuben the eldest to Ephraim the
    youngest,
From the firstborn to him who had been
    given
The richest blessings.

All were equal
In the lineages of the House of Israel,
Yet because of the ancient birthright
It was Ephraim who guided the people
Through the mountains.

Among these were the prophets
Who were now coming in from all over the
    land,
Bringing with them the ancient records
And the rich treasures of their people,

Bringing also a reassurance
That all was well
And that the Lord himself
Would deliver his people!

* * *

Finally,
At an appointed time,
When all the tribes had gathered together,
The signal once more was given
For the Camp of Israel to move.

Again our journey was northward,
Continuing on through the mountains
And along the canyons and gorges
Of the great river,

Threading our way slowly up the inclines
And over countless passes,
A long line of people stretching forward
    and backward
As far as the eye could see.

There was no dropping out along the way
As in olden times when another group
Began a northern journey.
Nothing else remained for us but to go
    ahead,
Always keeping the river as our guide.

The river was larger now
And continually at flood stage,
And even though our traveling was steadily
    upward,
The waters never seemed to decrease.

It became more and more obvious
In those days
That we were not following the usual kind
    of stream,
But instead a huge watercourse,
Fed by some giant unknown source ahead
    of us.

It was also apparent,
As the months went by,
That our environment had begun to change.
There was a difference in climate now,
And the sun was seldom seen
Because of the clouds.

Landforms and vegetation
Both took on a different appearance,
And wildlife virtually disappeared.

Without knowing what was taking place,
We eventually came to an understanding
That our long journey through the mountains
Would soon come to an end,
And that the valleys we were leaving
    behind us
Would be gone forever.

On the day
We no longer could hear the river,
We knew for certain
That the time was near.
The sound of water
Which had been close by for so many
    months
Suddenly vanished,
And a deep stillness filled the air.

It were as though
A new signal had been given,
One to prepare the people
For what was just ahead.

And as we journeyed farther
Into the mountains,
We were like the people of old following
    Moses,
Who came to the shores of the Red Sea
Wondering where they were going
And what might befall them.

                * * *

No one remembers exactly
What happened that day,
Only that we had congregated in a large
    valley
Surrounded by cliffs
And were again waiting for the time
    to move.

High above us
On a promontory of rocks,
The prophets were assembled
For a meeting.

A quietness
Still pervaded the atmosphere,
And despite the overcast of clouds
A brightness prevailed.

It was a peaceful day
When no one had any presentiment
That something so remarkable and
    extraordinary
Was about to take place.

And then suddenly,
And without warning, a sound occurred!
Later some said it was like a bell,
Others more like a siren or a woman
    screaming.
But it was a brief sound,
And immediately everyone looked
Toward the promontory above.

We were concerned about the prophets now
Because the cliffs were coming down,
And rocks everywhere were falling around
    them.
A huge avalanche of boulders and stones
Cascaded down the mountain,
And a blanket of dust covered the valley.

Some claimed there was thunder and
    lightning
While others thought they heard rifle fire
    and cannon.
Still it was difficult to know what happened
Because of the loud noise and confusion.

Yet the light continued,
And when the air cleared around us,
We could see the prophets beyond,
Walking through a large opening
In the cliffs,

Their arms and hands raised in front of them,
Smiting the rocks, as it were,
Striking down a veritable fortress of stone
And finally causing a sheet of whiteness
    to appear.

And as we followed them
Through the opening,
Marveling at all that was taking place,
We could then see the gigantic wall of ice
Which lay directly ahead.

Like an iron gate
That had been lowered to prevent our
    escape,
It now stood between us and the outside
    world
We had traveled so far to see.

This barrier of ice
The prophets also smote,
Using all the power and authority
Given to them by the fathers,
As well as the prophets of old.

And as a consequence
The ice moved slightly,
Then cracked and groaned,
And finally broke away
In large sheets,
Falling down before us,

Opening up a vista beyond
Of open water and floating icebergs,
An incredible scene of whiteness and
    sunshine
Which momentarily dimmed our vision
And blurred our view.

Then came the highway,
A long line of dry ground
Suddenly rising out of the depths
And parting the waters
Of the arctic sea!

A path of rescue
For the ransomed to pass over
And a way of holiness
To set the captives free,

It reached far ahead of us
Into the distance,
Pointing the way southward
Toward the place called Zion,
To a promised land
And the new Jerusalem,

Leading us to a haven
Of refuge and safety
Where finally we would fall down
Before our kinsmen of old,
There to be received in honor
And crowned with glory!

* * *

That evening,
After we had crossed to the mainland,
I walked alone
To a place outside Israel's camp.

My thoughts were not of myself
Or the ones who traveled with me,
But only of those who had stayed behind,
My wife and children and family.

Even now,
According to the prophets,
The deluge of the river
Had overcome them.

The waters of the great deep
Had flooded my homeland,
Covering every hill and valley
And restoring once again the ancient
    shorelines
Of the prehistoric sea.

These were my thoughts,
And I mourned for all those who were gone,
Those who did not listen to prophecy
And who ignored the signs upon the
    mountains.

For a time
Their haunting memory would not leave,
And I began to question
And doubt.

But then suddenly
There was a new thought
And a new feeling,
The reassurance that all was well
And that finally we were on our way
Toward Zion,

Leaving the mountains behind us,
And the land of ice and snow,
And heading toward a distant land,
A peaceful land
Of grass with reeds and rushes
And pools of living water.

And as I returned to camp that night,
I faced the future with a bright hope
And a new thanksgiving,
Resolving once more always to follow the
    prophets
And never again to turn and look back.

EPILOGUE

Two important questions which arise in connection with the ten tribes relate directly to the days of Peleg, the time period in which a third deluge allegedly took place. If such an event actually did happen, for example, why was there a large influx of water at this particular time in history, so close to the great Flood, and also what purpose did it serve by causing a division of the earth into islands and continents?

First of all, whatever the purpose might have been, it would seem that it could have been taken care of at the end of the Flood itself which had occurred only a hundred years before or, at the most, a few centuries earlier. Instead of all the water draining off in five and a half months, as suggested in the Book of Genesis, a lesser volume might have receded so that the earth ended up as it did during Peleg's time, with the right configuration of land and the correct amount of sea and ocean. At least this would have brought the number of floods down to two rather than three.

And although this idea is a definite possibility, things might not have happened that way! No clues are mentioned in the Bible as to why or why not, but there are good reasons for rejecting such a theory. (See Figure 16.) Also as to why the earth was divided, in the first place, there are no definite clues given for that either.

An important purpose of the division, however, could have been related to one of the most well-known events in the biblical record, namely the building of the Tower of Babel. In fact, because of the language involved, some believe that the confounding of tongues and the wide dispersion of people at that time, as recorded in the Genesis account, were exactly

Figure 16

The Number of Deluges

It is possible that the division of the earth was not a separate deluge by itself but merely the tail end, so to speak, of the great Flood in the days of Noah. In other words, when the Flood was over, the waters did not entirely subside but stopped at a point during Peleg's time which provided the network of islands and continents as they exist today.

Certainly this explanation would simplify things, such as avoiding the question as to why there were two large deluges so close to one another. But the easiest and most logical solution is not always the correct one, and in connection with the event pertaining to Peleg, this might very well be true.

There are at least three reasons, for example, why the division was one of three giant floods, separate and distinct from the other two:

(1) The wording in the biblical text suggests that this particular deluge was an event which occurred abruptly and independently. It was not merely the culmination of the great Flood. Otherwise, the text might have stated that during the days of Peleg, "the earth was finally divided" or that "the division of land became complete."

(2) If the division was the point at which the Flood completely came to an end, establishing the system of present-day islands and continents, the question arises as to how people in those days knew that such a point had been reached. The scriptural text, once again, implies a more distinct and observable event.

(3) The naming of Peleg also suggests a more definite occurrence. It strongly intimates that when he was born, something very remarkable took place. The division of the earth, in other words, was not just a situation in which geography changed gradually over a long period of time and was possibly unknown to most of the people, but an event that happened separately and attracted a great deal of interest and attention.

It was not a catastrophe like the deluge in the time of Noah, yet very possibly a flood scare nevertheless, one which might have caused considerable alarm among the people.

---

what the Bible was talking about when it said the earth was divided.

"These are the families of the sons of Noah," the record says, "after their generations, in their nations: and by these were the nations divided in the earth after the flood." [44]

The confusion arises in the fact that there were actually two types of divisions: the dividing of the nations and also the dividing of the earth, both taking place at about the same time. Each was related in its own way to the Tower of Babel, yet the two were definitely different occurrences.

Concerning the division of nations, the Bible is very explicit. "So the Lord scattered them abroad from thence upon the face of all the earth: and they left off to build the city. Therefore is the name of it called Babel, because the Lord did there confound the language of all the earth." [45]

Once again, however, this is not be confused with the division of the earth itself which resulted in the present-day geography of islands and continents. [46] And yet the two events still remain very closely related.

One of the reasons that the earth was divided during the days of Peleg was evidently to set the stage for an extensive division of population. Some of the people were scattered into adjacent land areas, but others were destined to go across the oceans and into the isles of the sea. And in order for the latter to occur, there needed to be a much greater amount of water.

The intent was apparently not only to section off various parts of the earth's surface in preparation for future migrations, but at the same time to keep certain people isolated from the rest of the world, for whatever reason. This was especially true of the people known as the Jaredites who, according to modern scripture, left the Tower of Babel during the confusion of tongues and began a long journey, possibly toward the east and across the Indian and Pacific Oceans, to establish a large civilization on the American Continent.

The Jaredite migration, which could have occurred around 2200 B.C., or maybe a few centuries earlier, implies that the division of the earth had already taken place, since oceans appear to have existed at that time where previously there had been mainly land. Actually, the huge influx of water might have been a type of signal that the hour had finally arrived for the journey to begin.

The departure of the Jaredites from the Near East during that early time period also was symbolic of things to come, a prelude, in a way, to the journeys of Abraham and the future dispersions of the House of Israel. An account of them leaving their homeland is very similar, in fact, to the apocryphal record of the ten tribes as they left their place of captivity for the north country.

"And it came to pass that the Lord commanded them (the Jaredites) that they should go forth into the wilderness, yea, into that quarter where there never had man been. And it came to pass that the Lord did go before them, and did talk with them as he stood in a cloud, and gave directions whither they should travel." [47]

In addition to the Jaredite migration and various others that took place down through history, there is still another possible reason why the earth was divided, one that involves some very unusual circumstances. It is the idea that the ten tribes were standing in the wings, as it were, waiting for their turn to come on stage and begin their own migration, and also biding their time until a land and destination could be prepared for them!

This means that at the time of the division, at a subterranean location in another department of the earth, a gigantic sea or ocean was divested of much of its water. The fountains of the great deep once more were broken up, causing floods to plunge to the surface and spread across large portions of the land. This was the deluge in the days of Peleg, and one of its main purposes could well have been to create living space for the ten tribes of Israel!

For most of the time during past ages, the fountains had lain dormant, serving no apparent purpose but to form a giant water supply to be used when needed. Allegedly, they had burst forth at the dawn of Creation, and definitely during the days of the Flood, and then again at a point in history when Peleg was born, they very possibly came to the surface a third time and caused the dramatic division of the earth.

Wherever such a large volume of water came from in those days, it undoubtedly left space there, not only a diminished sea or ocean but maybe hills and valleys as well. And as in the time of Noah following the great Flood, these land forms now began to dry out and during the centuries that followed were sculptured by the elements and tempered by a long passage of time.

Once again, whether or not any of this would be accepted by geologists and earth scientists, even as a remote possibility, is another matter. Certainly it would be understandable if they regarded it more as fiction than reality, also as an oversimplification, in some ways, of a very complex subject. Yet if it is true, or even close to the truth, it might help explain one of the most puzzling situations in biblical history--the disappearance and present location of the ten lost tribes of Israel!

A question that arises in regard to this kind of theory, however, pertains to the qualities of water. Does it have the capability, for example, of performing in the ways that such a theory requires? In other words, is it feasible that a tremendous amount of water could come up from a subterranean area, possibly by way of underground rivers and large fractures in the earth, and then emerge at a place in the north country to cover extensive areas of land?

One thing can be said for certain, and that is that during the world's history, water has come from somewhere, two and possibly three times, and caused a spectacular flood. In the first two instances, it has also gone back again, presumably to its original source, and in the future it will once more recede one last time.

It is also certain that such events do not occur merely by way of normal circumstances, or according to a natural explanation of things. They happen as the result of divine intervention and the issuance of a divine command.

A description of their occurrence is not likely to be recorded so much in geological terms, as in those that are scriptural. Such phrasing in the Bible as "the Spirit of God moved upon the face of the waters" is a good example, and also "the fountains of the great deep were broken up." And in modern scripture there is the same type of language, in one place especially where the words and phrases ring out not only as a prediction for the future but as type of forewarning as well.

"He shall command the great deep, and it shall be driven back into the north countries, and the islands shall become one land; and the land of Jerusalem and the land of Zion shall be turned back into their own place, and the earth shall be like as it was in the days before it was divided." [48]

The word *driven* in this last passage is particularly important. It describes water action in a way that is again typically scriptural. And whereas some might regard it as mainly a figurative expression, there is possibly much more to it than that.

A similar situation is found in the Book of Exodus. Before the children of Israel crossed over the Red Sea, the Lord caused a wind to blow for several hours during the night, dividing the waters and creating a pathway across dry land. This would indicate that the sea was literally driven back until there was a wall of water on both sides.

"And Moses stretched out his hand over the sea; and the Lord caused the sea to go back by a strong east wind all that night, and made the sea dry land, and the waters were divided. And the children of Israel went into the midst of the sea upon the dry ground; and the waters were a wall unto them on their right hand, and on their left." [49]

As to a quality of water, therefore, which would allow oceans and seas, as well as underground fountains or rivers, to be propelled forward and backward in an unorthodox manner, there is at least one good precedent for it in the Bible.

Another incident of the same kind, only on a much smaller scale, occurred at the time that Elijah was taken up into heaven. Just prior to this event, he and Elisha came to the Jordan River, and in order to get across, Elijah smote the waters with his mantle, dividing them so they could walk through on dry ground. A short time later, Elisha recrossed the river in the same way, using Elijah's mantle which had been left behind. [50]

It was a very small thing compared to what Moses had done, but again it demonstrates an unusual aspect of water, especially in relation to a divine command. And along with the incident pertaining to the Red Sea, it substantiates the idea that the flood which might have taken place during the days of Peleg came from an underground sea or ocean, the water literally being gathered together and driven to the earth's surface.

Finally, there is the idea that the deluge in Peleg's time, coming as it did out of the north country, was related in some way to the region in which the ten tribes disappeared. Floodwaters, in other words, could have emerged somewhere in the vicinity of where a large migration of people later entered a subterranean area.

And just as the ancient tribes went in where the waters had come out, the opposite might happen in the future, the original place of entry becoming an exit and the floodwaters returning at the same place. Also a route once followed by the tribes into an unknown region might possibly be retraced many hundreds of years later by their descendants, far removed in time and the number of generations.

It will be this last event, therefore, the return of the lost tribes, that will be particularly impressive. Their reappearance at a future date, after so many centuries of seclusion, will undoubtedly be the scene of almost unbelievable circumstances. The prediction of a dramatic encounter with rock and ice, along with the sudden highway in the midst of the sea, heralds this event as one of the most important and incredible in the world's history.

And after everything that has occurred in connection with this remarkable race of people, anything less would be an anticlimax and a contradiction!

Figure 17

Sea Levels After the Floods and Recessions

Two times in history, and maybe three, a large influx of water has come in upon the earth. This occurred during the Creation, at the time of the Flood, and possibly in the days of Peleg. (A, B, and C)

In the first two instances, much of the water later receded, evidently going back to its original source. A third recession, according to religious prophecy, will take place sometime in the last days just prior to the Millennium. (1, 2, and 3)

The diagram below gives only a general idea as to the possible sea levels involved and does not suggest any kind of accuracy in regard to time or space.

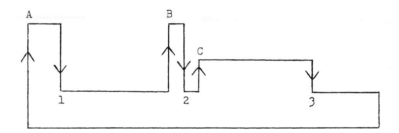

After the first gathering of waters, according to this theory, the seas were much smaller than at present, and the land was joined together in one place. This same condition existed following the Flood.

In the time of Peleg, however, the amount of water once more increased and created the large seas and oceans as they exist today. These will continue until the Millennium, at which time the land surfaces of the globe will again revert to the way they were in the beginning.

REFERENCES AND COMMENTS

Note: *The King James Version of the Bible, The Book of Mormon, The Doctrine and Covenants,* and *The Pearl of Great Price* are standard works of the Church of Jesus Christ of Latter-Day Saints.

1. Genesis 1:2, 9-10.

2. Ibid., 7:11, 24 and 8:2-3.

3. Another explanation of what might have occurred is the rising terrain theory. If the ocean floor were raised up, for example, it would displace a large amount of water onto land surfaces. Conversely, sinking terrain would cause the water to drain off again.

4. Doctrine and Covenants 133:23.

5. Ibid., 133:38-39. See also Revelation 14:7.

6. Genesis 10:25. See also I Chronicles 1:19.

7. Doctrine and Covenants 133:23-24.

8. Proverbs 8:22-24, 27-29.

9. There are many things in the Apocrypha that have been declared to be true, along with things that are not true. (See Doctrine and Covenants 91:1-2.) The account pertaining to the ten tribes has often been used as a source of information but has not yet been completely verified.

10. II Esdras 13:41-45. See Bruce M. Metzger (Editor), *The Apocrypha of the Old Testament,* Revised Standard Version (New York: Oxford University Press, 1965), p. 65.

11. Doctrine and Covenants 133:23, 26-27.

12. Jeremiah 16:14-15. See also 23:7-8.

13. R. Clayton Brough, *The Lost Tribes* (Salt Lake City: Horizon Publishers, 1979), p. 44.

14. Doctrine and Covenants 133:26-27.

15. Isaiah 35:7-8.

16. Doctrine and Covenants 133:22, 28-29. See also Isaiah 35:7-10.

17. Revelation 5:13.

18. Philippians 2:9-11.

19. Book of Moses 6:63. See The Pearl of Great Price.

20. Raymond Bernard, *The Hollow Earth* (Secaucus, New Jersey: University Books, Incorporated, 1969).

21. Seiya Uyeda, *The New View of the Earth* (San Francisco: W.H. Freeman and Company, 1978), p. 186.

22. A. Hallum, *A Revolution in the Earth Sciences* (Oxford: Clarendon Press, 1973), p. 113.

23. Moses 7:48. See The Pearl of Great Price.

24. Matthew 12:40.

25. I Kings 11:31, 35-36.

26. Ibid., 14:15.

27. II Kings 15:29 and I Chronicles 5:26.

28. H.R. Hall, *The Ancient History of the Near East* (London: Methuen and Company, 1913), p. 466. Others have also

expressed this same view, pointing out that only a part of a conquered area was taken into captivity.

29. II Kings 17:5-6. Shalmaneser V is sometimes referred to as the one who conquered Samaria. The likelihood, however, is that his rule ended in about 722 B.C., and the conquest of the city occurred one year later.

30. Hall, op. cit., p. 474. The Assyrians were well-known for their war atrocities, and although the biblical record makes no mention of it, there were undoubtedly many casualties during the invasions.

31. Andre Parrot, *Samaria, the Capital of the Kingdom of Israel* (New York: Philosophical Library, Incorporated, 1958), p. 51. Note: The number of captives usually mentioned in other texts, and the one that appears to be correct, is 27,290.

32. II Kings 17:23-24.

33. John 10:16.

34. III Nephi 17:4. See The Book of Mormon.

35. Ibid., 21:26, 28 Note: Scriptural references to Israelites being in the north country or the land of the north apparently included other groups besides the lost tribes. Eventually, all of these people will "be gathered home to the land of their inheritance."

36. II Nephi 29:12-13. See The Book of Mormon.

37. Doctrine and Covenants 133:30-31.

38. Robert Edwin Peary, *The North Pole* (New York: Frederick A. Stokes Company, 1910), pp. 196-97.

39. Ibid., pp. 74-75.

40. Doctrine and Covenants 133:32.

41. Jeremiah was another prophet who referred to the Kingdom of Israel as *Ephraim*. In prophesying against Judah, he gave them the following words of warning from the Lord: "And I will cast you out of my sight, as I have cast out all your brethren, even the whole seed of Ephraim." (Jeremiah 7:15)

42. Joseph Smith, *History of the Church of Jesus Christ of Latter-Day Saints* (Salt Lake City, Utah: Deseret Book Company, 1951), Vol. I, p. 315.

43. Doctrine and Covenants 133:21, 24-25.

44. Genesis 10:32.

45. Ibid., 11:8-9.

46. Genesis 10:25 and I Chronicles 1:19.

47. Ether 2:5. See The Book of Mormon.

48. Doctrine and Covenants 133:23-24.

49. Exodus 14:21-22.

50. II Kings 2:8-14.

GENERALIZATIONS

1. Believing in miraculous occurrences requires not only an act of intellect but also the exercise of faith.

2. One of the good things about being a Christian is that there are so many miracles to believe in, and many which are still to come.

3. The more unbelievable a phenomenon or event might appear sometimes, the more potential it could actually have of being true and significant.

4. Whenever possible, it is a good idea to look for a natural explanation of things, going along with science instead of refuting it.

5. Events and physical phenomena which are of great magnitude and which significantly affect the lives of many people do not always happen by chance, or according to natural causes, but might occur at a specific time and place as the result of a divine command.

6. A lack of knowledge and information can easily result in bothersome questions, and the only way to get rid of them, if that is possible, is to try to find the answers, or at least form an enlightened opinion supported by the facts that are available and the best of circumstantial evidence.

7. A good way to lose credibility sometimes while talking about events pertaining to religion is to attribute too many things to miracles or divine intervention.

8. Radically new concepts often gain acceptance very slowly, if at all.

9. The survival of a new idea is especially difficult when controversy is involved.

10. Any solution or explanation of a problem that is too simplistic might run the risk of not being true at all.

11. Scientific discovery is an ongoing process, and what is regarded as correct today could quickly change tomorrow.

12. Just as something plausible might turn out to be false, something that appears unreasonable might eventually end up being true.

13. A theory which is considered to be scientifically sound could potentially be very tentative and insecure.

14. An idea held in derision because it is different and revolutionary might only have to bide its time before experiencing success.

15. Some subjects, because of their nature, are difficult to explain and consequently have to be considered within a very different context and set of circumstances.

16. Things might appear unrealistic and hard to believe yet at the same time be in harmony with general Christian practice and tradition.

17. Casually refuting large amounts of evidence which modern science has produced is never an educated thing to do.

18. The use of intellect is often separate from the exercise of faith, and unless a person is sensitive to both, he or she might mistakenly neglect one principle in favor of the other.

19. While some people rely heavily on science for answers, with very little knowledge of religion, others do just the opposite, and the unfortunate thing sometimes is that

the two groups cannot be more tolerant and patient with one another.

20. During the research process where a competition of ideas exists, there is often a controversial atmosphere in which opinions are explored and theories are tested, but in the end, truth usually prevails, even though it might have been unpopular along the way.